The Challenge of Indigenous Education:
Practice and Perspectives

The designations employed and the presentation of
material throughout this publication do not imply the
expression of any opinion whatsoever on the part of
UNESCO concerning the legal status of any country,
territory, city or area or of its authorities, or concerning
the delimitation of its frontiers or boundaries.

The authors are responsible for the choice and the
presentation of the facts contained in this book and
for the opinions expressed therein, which are not
necessarily those of UNESCO and do not commit the
Organization.

Published in 2004 by the
United Nations Educational,
Scientific and Cultural Organization
7, place de Fontenoy F-75352 Paris 07 SP
Typeset by IGS-CP - 16340 L'Isle-d'Espagnac
Printed by Jouve, Mayenne

ISBN 92-3-103934-2

Printed in France

THE CHALLENGE OF INDIGENOUS EDUCATION: PRACTICE AND PERSPECTIVES

Linda King and Sabine Schielmann

Education on the move

UNESCO PUBLISHING

PREFACE

Education is one of the six mandated areas of the United Nations Permanent Forum on Indigenous Issues and an area on which we have much to say. The Third Session of the Forum in 2004 will devote a good deal of time to education and culture, in addition to human rights, and this publication will make an important contribution to that debate.

I was an indigenous child myself once – a long time ago. I would like you to come with me on a journey and to imagine the life experience of the indigenous child. You arrive at school with a rich cultural background only to find out that there is an expectation that you should have already accessed pre-school education. But of course you had no access to such things – even access to basic education is a luxury.

On your first day you discover that the teachers do not speak your language, in fact, they don't even want you to speak your language. You may even be punished for doing so. The teachers know nothing of your culture; they say 'look at me when I speak to you', but in your culture it may be disrespectful to look at adults directly. Day by day you are torn between two worlds. You look through your many textbooks but find no reflection of yourself, your family or your culture. Even in the history books your people are invisible. They exist only in the shadows – or worse, if they are mentioned at all it is as 'obstacles to settlement' or simply as 'problems' for your country to overcome.

But children are tough and somehow you survive in this environment. However, you notice as you reach secondary school that many of your indigenous brothers and sisters have dropped out. Did they fail school or did school fail them? By senior high school you are the only one left. The teachers say 'but you are not like the others', but in your heart you know that you are.

All too often this is the educational experience of indigenous children – those who have the luxury of access to formal schooling. Many do not. In the Second Session of the Permanent Forum in 2003, many indigenous representatives discussed common education issues including poor retention and attainment and graduation rates throughout the compulsory and non-compulsory years of schooling. Many also discussed overt and systemic racism and marginalization as root causes of educational underachievement faced by indigenous young people. Some representatives emphasized the link between access to and success in early childhood education and ongoing success in later schooling and life.

Indigenous communities face many challenges in education. We live in a world that is increasingly multicultural, and the traditional understand-ing of the content of curricula and ways of teaching, even for those states that are organized on the assumption that they are culturally homogenous (Rodolfo Stavenhagen has coined the term 'ethnocratic' for these kind of states), simply does not work anymore. The world is more uncertain than ever before, as observed both by the World Commission on Culture and Development (the De Cuéllar Commission) and the International Commis-sion on Education for the Twenty-First Century (the Delors Commission). Furthermore, indigenous peoples and minorities are largely ignored in most countries in both the design of curricula and the organization of teaching. In fact, in many countries the basic principles of multilingual and multicul-tural education as established by UNESCO have been barely implemented. And lastly, there is always the question of resources. We are poorest among the poor. Even in developed countries, indigenous communities are not able to offer their children adequate education – and especially not an education that meets the aspirations of the peoples themselves.

But indigenous peoples do not come only with problems that need solving – we come with our own answers and ask your assistance in ensur-ing these solutions are systematically and fully implemented. Quality in education is not an absolute and static concept, because education relates to the culture and community it is supposed to serve. The aspirations of the world's indigenous peoples in the field of education is so far best reflected in Article 15 of The United Nations Draft Declaration on the Rights of Indigenous Peoples:

Indigenous children have the right to all levels and forms of education of the State. All indigenous peoples also have this right and the right to establish and control their educational systems and institutions providing education in their own languages, in a manner appropriate to their cultural methods of teaching and learning.

Indigenous children living outside their communities have the right to be provided access to education in their own culture and language.

Our cultures and our knowledge must be included in the curricula for indigenous children and youth at all levels of education. There is no quality in an education where everything is based on a culture other than ours. Our cultures have a rich reservoir of knowledge. We want to preserve and develop this – and we want to share it for the benefit of all human kind. For indigenous peoples, it is the knowledge of the interconnectedness of all that was, that is and that will be – the vast mosaic of life and spirit and land/water forms, of which we are an intricate part. It encompasses all that is known as Traditional Knowledge.

Indigenous cultural heritage involves a holistic approach, where traditions and knowledge are embodied in songs, stories and designs as well as in the land and the environment – the intangible interlinked with the tangible. For Indigenous peoples, sacred sites and intangible cultural heritage are intimately woven together and cannot be easily separated. These allow us to balance development with our environment, which we have occupied since time immemorial. This knowledge indeed forms the central pillars of our culture; pillars that also sustain the Earth. Deviation from this knowledge has grave consequences for the world and for human kind.

But we do not want to limit ourselves to our own knowledge. We want to combine the best of our own traditions with the best of Western and European traditions. This is quality in a true sense.

The United Nations Special Rapporteur on the Situation of Human Rights and Fundamental Freedoms of Indigenous Peoples, Mr. Rodolfo Stavenhagen, has pointed out that our 'cultural specificies are also contributions to a universal culture and not mere relics of a disappearing past'. This means that elements from our cultures and our knowledge should be included within education for other peoples as well as our own.

Traditional indigenous education and its structures should be respected and supported. Our knowledge has not been written down by us – on the contrary: we dance it, we draw it, we narrate it, we sing it, we practise it. There is a need for a deeper understanding of what knowledge and learning are and the many paths that lead to them. This is in line with what was observed by the Delors Commission: Western formal education systems tend to emphasize the acquisition of knowledge to the detriment of other types of learning (UNESCO, 1997). I believe that indigenous peoples can contribute significantly both to our own education systems and to the renewal of education systems of other peoples.

We need to:

- establish effective arrangements for the participation of indigenous parents and community members in decisions regarding the planning, delivery and evaluation of education services for their children, young people and other community members
- increase the number of indigenous people employed as education administrators, teachers, coaches, curriculum advisers, teachers assistants, home-school liaison officers and other education workers, including community people engaged in teaching indigenous culture, history and contemporary society, and indigenous languages
- provide education and training services to develop the skills of indigenous people to participate in educational decision-making
- develop arrangements for the provisions of independent advice from indigenous communities regarding educational decisions at all levels, and
- achieve the participation of indigenous children, young people and adults in education for a period similar to that for other students.

We must ensure that indigenous children, young people and adults have access to all levels of education (including adult education) on a basis comparable to that available to other citizens.

We must enable indigenous students to attain skills and graduation rates to the same standard as other students throughout the compulsory and non-compulsory schooling years.

We must further:

- Develop programmes to support the maintenance and continued use of indigenous languages. Every individual should have a right to her or his own language, one of the national languages and an international language. Language teaching should be based on the results of research and UNESCO recommendations in this field (UNESCO has recently published a Position Paper: 'Education in a Multilingual World' UNESCO, 2003.

- Develop writing systems for indigenous languages. Writing is a basic skill for learning and a prerequisite for preserving and developing a language.
- Ensure that our languages are used in teaching, research and administration. The use of a language in different fields of society is the most efficient way of developing a language.

We need to provide community education services that will enable indigenous people to develop the skills to manage the development of their communities.

We further need to promote anti-racism education, including strategies to empower young people to deal with racism in the compulsory schooling curriculum.

Indigenous peoples should be resourced and supported to establish their own education systems, including schools, should they so choose.

The right to preserve and develop our own reservoir of knowledge is a fundamental aspect of self-determination. This resource is equally important to the 'natural wealth and resources' referred to in the human rights conventions (cf, The United Nations International Covenant on Civil and Political Rights, Art. 1). We have a collective right to determine our own path of development. For that purpose, we need a firm basis of knowledge on the consequences of our choices and decisions. Education is the door to new knowledge. Therefore, education cannot be limited only to primary and secondary education. Higher education and research are a necessary source both to society at large and as a basis for the education system itself.

These are some of the strategies that we believe, if fully and effectively implemented, will lead to equitable educational attainment for indigenous children and young people.

The Dakar Education For All (EFA) goals, although drawing attention to our problems in its first three aims, do not highlight the specificity of indigenous people's education:

1. Expanding and improving comprehensive early childhood care and education, especially for the most vulnerable and disadvantaged children.
2. Ensuring that by 2015 all children, particularly girls, children in difficult circumstances and those belonging to ethnic minorities, have

   access to and complete free and compulsory primary education of
   good quality.

3. Ensuring that the learning needs of all young people and adults are
   met through equitable access to appropriate learning and life skills
   programmes.

I want to stress that we are not simply either 'living in difficult circumstances'
or 'ethnic minorities'. We are the original inhabitants of our traditional lands
and waters – we are proudly 'indigenous'. I ask that we all strive together to
ensure that indigenous peoples are visible and that we participate in matters
that affect us. Most of all we must ensure that these goals are achieved for
indigenous children.

   Quality in education for indigenous peoples means that our education,
in principle, is based on our own culture, our knowledge, our own languages
and learning/teaching traditions. From this platform indigenous peoples will
be able to reach for the best in the global garden of knowledge.* This book
is one step in the right direction.

Mr. Ole Henrik Magga
President of the United Nations Permanent
Forum on Indigenous Issues

---

* Cf. Amartya Sen, *Culture, Economics and Development*, a paper contributed to the World
Commission on Culture and Development in May 1995. See also Mahbub ul Haq, 1995
Reflections on Human Development, New York and Oxford, Oxford University Press and
UNESCO, 1996, *Our Creative Diversity*, p. 22.

CONTENTS

INTRODUCTION

There are indigenous peoples living in many countries, all over the world.[1] They include the Indians of the Americas, the Inuit and Aleutians of the circumpolar region, the Saami of northern Europe, the Aborigines of Australia, the Maori of New Zealand, and other peoples spread across the world, from the Arctic to the South Pacific. There are about 5,000 different indigenous and tribal peoples, numbering about 300 million individuals altogether.[2] It is estimated that about 4,000 to 5,000 of the more than 6,000 languages still spoken in the world are spoken by indigenous peoples.[3] Indigenous peoples live in widely varying environments, many in rural areas, and most have retained their specific cultural identity, languages, customs and traditions, social organization, economy, practices and spiritual beliefs.

Acknowledging indigenous peoples' specific situation and their unique contributions, as well as the problems they face in the context of today's multicultural and multilingual societies, the United Nations World Conference on Human Rights, held in Vienna in 1993, recommended the proclamation of an International Decade of the World's Indigenous People, a motion that was subsequently approved by the UN General Assembly in 1994.[4] The Programme of activities for the International Decade (1995 to 2004) adopted by the General Assembly stated that:

> The main objective of the International Decade of the World's Indigenous People is the strengthening of international co-operation for the solution of

problems faced by indigenous people in such areas as human rights, the
environment, development, health, culture and education.[5]

This study is a contribution to the United Nations International Decade and
addresses some of the issues highlighted during the second session of the
UN Permanent Forum on Indigenous Issues held in May 2003, in particular
the discrimination suffered by indigenous peoples in the education system,
the loss of indigenous languages, the exclusion of indigenous cultures and
knowledge in school curricula, and the need to promote the participation
and contribution of indigenous peoples in the development of culturally and
linguistically appropriate educational programmes.[6]

Education for indigenous people is as diverse as the cultures and
societies in which indigenous people live, and a wide range of educational
approaches and programmes currently exist throughout the world. This
document provides an overview of different experiences in indigenous education and points to some of the specific concerns of indigenous peoples, as
well as to their contribution to quality education. The term 'indigenous
education' does not refer to a different, exclusive or parallel category of
education, but rather emphasizes the need to address indigenous peoples'
specific needs in order to raise awareness and broaden the scope of discussion
with a view to achieving quality education for all.

Case studies illustrating good practice in education for indigenous
peoples are included in the final part of the document. The intention is not
to prescribe certain models for direct application or transfer, but to show a
range of educational programmes that reflect the diversity of the cultural,
linguistic and geographic circumstances of indigenous peoples, in addition
to their educational needs and goals.

Education for indigenous peoples cannot be considered in isolation
from issues of poverty, democracy and human rights. Article 6 of the World
Declaration on Education for All states that successful learning can only take
place in healthy and culturally appropriate environments and when learning
is connected to other aspects of life and to the well-being of the learner.
Indigenous education is, furthermore, situated within the context of
contemporary discussions on cultural, linguistic and biological diversity
and their interrelation, as well as associated issues of identity, survival
and sustainability.

Education is both a prerequisite to, and a tool for, enhancing the
opportunities of learners to exercise their social, cultural, economic, civil
and political rights. Education for indigenous peoples needs therefore to be

considered on the basis of recognition and understanding, and the promotion of human rights, specific cultural identity, and the contribution of indigenous peoples to plural societies.

Part I of this study reflects upon the challenges and obstacles facing indigenous education, the situation of indigenous peoples with regard to education, aspects of the political and legal context, and prospects for indigenous education. It also summarizes the general objectives of indigenous education. Part II develops a set of criteria for the identification of successful examples of quality education for indigenous peoples, illustrated by some relevant experiences. Part III presents some successful case studies in education for indigenous peoples.

Dörthe Bühmann, Maria Luisa Jauregui, Ingrid Jung, Juan C. Godenzzi, Ulises Márquez Nava, Julio Murrieta, Alejandra Perez Reguerra, and Martha Pastor Escobar are gratefully acknowledged for their helpful comments on an early draft.

PART I.
CHALLENGES
AND OBSTACLES
IN INDIGENOUS
EDUCATION

I. 1
INDIGENOUS PEOPLES
AND EDUCATION

'Millions of people are still denied their right to education',[7] and indigenous peoples are among the most affected and disadvantaged. Their situation has often been characterized by a lack of access to an education that respects their diverse cultures and languages. Educational materials providing accurate and fair information on indigenous peoples and their ways of life have been all too rare, and, moreover, history textbooks have frequently depicted them in negative terms. Similarly, in many cases educational programmes have failed to offer indigenous peoples the possibility of participating in decision-making, the design of curricula, the selection of teachers and teaching methods, and the definition of standards.

The Programme of activities for the United Nations International Decade of the World's Indigenous People states:

> 3. A major objective of the Decade is education of indigenous and non-indigenous societies concerning the situation, cultures, languages, rights and aspirations of indigenous people.... 4. An objective of the Decade is the promotion and protection of the rights of indigenous people, and their empowerment to make choices that enable them to retain their cultural identity while participating in political, economic and social life, with full respect for their cultural values, languages, traditions and forms of social organization.[8]

Indigenous education however faces a double challenge:

- to support and promote the maintenance, use and survival of indigenous peoples' cultures, languages, knowledge, traditions and identity, and
- to provide and develop the knowledge and skills that enable indigenous peoples to participate fully and equally in the national and international community.

According to indigenous peoples' own view, the key issues in indigenous education are expressed in the following statement:

'We, the Indigenous people of the world, assert our inherent right to self-determination in all matters. Self-determination is about making informed choices and decisions. It is about creating appropriate structures for the transmission of culture, knowledge and wisdom for the benefit of each of our respective cultures. Education for our communities and each individual is central to the preservation of our cultures and for the development of the skills and expertise we need in order to be a vital part of the twenty-first century.'[9]

I. 2
LEGAL AND POLITICAL CONTEXT OF INDIGENOUS EDUCATION

There are a number of international instruments and declarations, as well as regional agreements in place today, which together comprise a basic framework for the provision of quality education for indigenous peoples and the recognition of their rights to education. [10]

Education is a fundamental human right, as enshrined in the Universal Declaration of Human Rights and reaffirmed in the World Declaration on Education for All and The Dakar Framework for Action. [11] The commitment of the international community to the provision of quality education to meet the basic learning needs of all children, youth and adults of today's culturally and linguistically diverse societies is clearly expressed within these international normative instruments.

The right of indigenous peoples to have access to education has often been mistakenly interpreted as meaning that indigenous peoples only want access to non-indigenous education. Yet indigenous peoples across the world are demanding educational provision that is both linguistically and culturally appropriate to their needs while not excluding them from broader access to national education systems. At the same time, education needs to be empowering and to draw from indigenous culture and wisdom. [12]

Article 18 of the Hamburg Declaration on Adult Learning expresses this idea as follows:

> Indigenous education and culture: Indigenous peoples and nomadic peoples have the right of access to all levels and forms of education provided by the

state. However, they are not to be denied the right to enjoy their own culture, or to use their own languages. Education for indigenous peoples and nomadic peoples should be linguistically and culturally appropriate to their needs and should facilitate access to further education and training.

The political and legal environment is a key factor. This requires:

- Constitutional recognition of the multicultural and multilingual nature of a society.
- Respect for and recognition of cultural and linguistic diversity.
- The guarantee of the basic human rights and fundamental freedoms of indigenous peoples, in particular recognizing that 'explicit and equal recognition of the diverse identities of the cultural and ethnic groups within a society is a basis for enabling members of these groups to access information and resources, and to fully develop their potential to achieve well-being as citizens'. [13]

Some countries constitutionally recognize indigenous peoples' rights to education, language and culture or have adopted specific laws regarding culturally appropriate education for indigenous peoples and the use of indigenous languages. Several Latin-American countries – Colombia, Mexico, Ecuador, Peru and Paraguay, for example – have reformed their constitutions in order to recognize the multi-ethnic, multicultural and multilingual character of their societies, and some of them have also established and/or institutionalized Intercultural Bilingual Education. The ratification of ILO Convention 169 is another important legislative step in this regard.

Other countries have responded to the specific situation and needs of indigenous peoples through the development of educational reforms or specific legislation on indigenous peoples and/or on education and mother-tongue instruction, such as the United States, the Philippines, Ecuador or Malaysia. [14]

The ILO Convention No. 169 on Indigenous and Tribal Peoples addresses indigenous education in Part VI and states in Article 26:

> Measures shall be taken to ensure that members of the peoples concerned have the opportunity to acquire education at all levels on at least an equal footing with the rest of the national community.

Article 27.1 of ILO Convention 169 specifies some characteristics of such measures:

> Education programmes and services for the peoples concerned shall be developed and implemented in co-operation with them and address their special needs, and shall incorporate their histories, their knowledge and technologies, their value systems and their further social, economic and cultural aspirations.

Such measures also include the provision of financial resources as an important factor for the success and sustainability of quality education for indigenous peoples. In particular, the possibilities for indigenous learners to access educational facilities of secondary and higher education for further learning are often limited principally due to costs. Furthermore, initiatives by indigenous and non-governmental organizations and indigenous communities themselves face threats to continuity because of lack of funding even though several international instruments support the establishment of indigenous peoples' own educational institutions and facilities.[15] In this regard, Article 27.3 of ILO Convention 169 points out:

> In addition, governments shall recognise the right of these peoples to establish their own educational institutions and facilities, provided that such institutions meet minimum standards established by the competent authority in consultation with these peoples. Appropriate resources shall be provided for this purpose.

However, despite positive legislative developments during the past two decades and an increasing recognition of indigenous peoples' educational and linguistic rights, much remains to be done to translate this legislation into policy and practice and to make this an education for all indigenous peoples, taking into account the fundamental role that education plays in empowering people and transforming societies.

I. 3
PERSPECTIVES
FOR INDIGENOUS EDUCATION

Current trends in 'Education for All' towards decentralizing and diversifying the provision of education, as well as innovative approaches in the field of intercultural bilingual education and the establishment of indigenous peoples' own educational programmes and institutions, are mutually reinforcing factors offering new perspectives for indigenous education.

The six goals set out for 'Education for All' by the Dakar Framework for Action are important to indigenous education. They focus on:

1. comprehensive early childhood care and education
2. free and compulsory primary education of good quality
3. equitable access to appropriate learning and life skills programmes
4. the improvement of adult literacy
5. the elimination of gender disparities
6. recognized and measurable learning outcomes.

In the context of indigenous education, the development of appropriate policies, strategies and programmes, and diverse, responsive and participatory approaches to meet these goals involves, among other factors:

*   reinforcing community-based practices of early childhood care
*   using local languages for initial literacy
*   creating culturally responsive programmes of bilingual – or multi-lingual – education for children and adults

- providing skills specific to indigenous cultures, such as hunting, trapping and weaving, as well as more general skills, knowledge, attitudes, values and beliefs of a wider diffusion [16]
- creating the basis and providing equal opportunities for further learning
- developing appropriate learning material
- using methods such as distance education, radio-broadcasting and e-learning, as well as creating in-situ programmes and training and employing local teachers to meet the needs of remote communities [17]
- linking education to other aspects of the learner's life, such as health, nutrition, safe water and the natural environment [18]
- using and integrating formal and non-formal learning styles and teaching methods as a means of recognizing indigenous ways of generating and transmitting knowledge and of giving value to the oral wisdom of indigenous peoples and non-verbal communication in education. [19]

This last point is underlined in the Action Plan for the Implementation of the UNESCO Universal Declaration on Cultural Diversity (2001), paragraph 8:

> Incorporating, where appropriate, traditional pedagogies into the education process with a view to preserving and making full use of culturally appropriate methods of communication and transmission of knowledge.

One of the approaches addressing the challenges of indigenous education is intercultural bilingual education. The concept of intercultural education goes beyond the recognition of the existence of more than one culture in a society; it promotes cross-cultural understanding and the integration of different languages and systems of learning and teaching.

Intercultural education is essentially a dialogue between different cultures, languages and concepts of knowledge, in which the educational rights and needs of different population groups are respected without discrimination. Indigenous representatives participating at the First Hemispheric Conference on Indigenous Education indicated that intercultural bilingual education best reflects their educational goals and values because it allows them to bring their cultural values and languages into the curriculum and promotes tolerance of other cultures and viewpoints. [20] UNESCO supports intercultural education as a means of promoting respect for cultural and linguistic diversity, encouraging understanding between different population groups and eliminating discrimination. [21]

Characteristics of intercultural bilingual or multilingual education include:

- recognizing and involving various cultural systems
- learning and teaching in more than one language, including the mother tongue, the official language(s) as well as international languages
- teacher training which is responsive to cultural and linguistic diversity
- inclusion and/or fusion of Western and indigenous educational and knowledge systems
- provision of knowledge and of tools that promote exchange, reciprocity and solidarity between, and living together of, different cultures and peoples. [22]

The Lima Declaration from the 2002 Regional Congress on Intercultural Bilingual Education states:

> It is necessary to generalize an intercultural education for all, and guarantee an intercultural bilingual basic education for all the indigenous populations [in Latin America]. [23]

However, despite its advantages and sustainability, intercultural education faces a number of problems. Some support the view that a monolingual and multicultural curriculum is most suitable for overcoming poverty and discrimination against minority groups. Others however argue in favour of a monocultural indigenous education, where the content and delivery of curricula are the responsibility of the indigenous community. [24]

Experiences from the United States, Canada, New Zealand, Australia and Bolivia point to the advantages of programmes co-ordinated by indigenous peoples in terms of strengthening instruction in indigenous languages; cultural revitalization; and survival, identity and self-esteem, and of enhancing ownership, responsibility and independence, as well as the continuity and sustainability of programmes. [25]

Recognizing and valuing diverse cultures, languages and knowledge systems in education (whether they be indigenous or non-indigenous) as equally valid helps to avoid the creation of a hierarchy of languages and knowledge systems and is essential in providing equal opportunities to education for all. [26]

I. 4
GENERAL OBJECTIVES
OF INDIGENOUS EDUCATION

To summarize the key issues regarding indigenous education highlighted above, some of the general objectives of providing quality education for indigenous peoples can be described as follows:

*   To ensure that indigenous peoples have equal access to, and the opportunity to reach, the same level of education as other citizens of the national community, including in higher education
*   To strengthen identities as a basis for promoting tolerance, understanding, peace and justice among cultures, and respect for cultural and linguistic diversity
*   To recognize, respect and integrate the cultural values, histories, languages, knowledge, traditions, customs – and specific relation to the land – of indigenous peoples in the design of educational programmes, policies and curricula
*   To enable indigenous peoples to take their rightful place in, and participate fully as members of, the local, national and global community, on the basis of their informed choices and decisions
*   To strengthen partnerships with indigenous peoples and their communities as a fundamental factor in the sustainability of programmes and policies, and
*   To recognize and strengthen the ownership of indigenous peoples over their own knowledge and education systems, and to recognize the

potential contribution of these systems to the promotion and advancement of culturally and linguistically appropriate quality education for all.

Part II.
CRITERIA FOR THE IDENTIFICATION OF GOOD PRACTICE IN INDIGENOUS EDUCATION

'Successful education programmes require: (1) healthy, well-nourished and motivated students; (2) well-trained teachers and active learning techniques; (3) adequate facilities and learning materials; (4) a relevant curriculum that can be taught and learned in a local language and builds upon the knowledge and experience of the teachers and learners; (5) an environment that not only encourages learning but is welcoming, gender-sensitive, healthy and safe; (6) a clear definition and accurate assessment of learning outcomes, including knowledge, skills, attitudes and values; (7) participatory governance and management; and (8) respect for and engagement with local communities and cultures.' [27]

A set of criteria focusing on specific issues relevant to indigenous programmes has been selected to identify key elements of good practice in indigenous education. These criteria include:

* Participation and decision-making
* Pedagogy and methodology
* Indigenous knowledge
* Curriculum
* Languages of instruction
* Teacher training
* Materials
* Assessment and evaluation.

II. 1
PARTICIPATION
AND DECISION-MAKING

Participation is a fundamental principle to ensure that the educational demands of indigenous peoples are heard. ILO Convention 169 emphasizes, in Article 27.1:

> Education programmes and services for the peoples concerned shall be developed and implemented *in cooperation with them* to address their special needs. (Emphasis added by the editor/author.)

The participation of indigenous communities in all stages of the design, implementation and evaluation of an educational programme is vital to its success and has various forms. It includes these communities' involvement in the elaboration and determination of teaching methods, curricula, material and school calendars, as well as in the appointment of teachers. The participation and support of parents is particularly important in early childhood care and primary education, as learning in and through the mother tongue is improved when the language is spoken at home. [28]

Another important aspect of participation is the involvement of indigenous elders as holders of traditional knowledge and speakers of the indigenous language. This can be facilitated through intergenerational learning programmes that involve both young and old in teaching and curriculum development, in formal as well as non-formal educational settings. [29]

Efforts should be made to have representation of indigenous communities at all levels of decision-making and administration in order to promote participation by indigenous peoples. This may include, for example, indigenous representation in school boards and policy-making committees as well as in institutions of the state education system. It further includes indigenous participation in the production, review and approval of educational material, especially when this material is produced in indigenous languages and/or contains information on indigenous knowledge.

Quality indigenous education fully and effectively involves indigenous peoples – in particular their elders, community leaders and parents – at all levels and stages of decision-making, planning, design and implementation of education programmes. This can be realized through:

- participatory processes to elaborate and determine teaching methods, curricula, material and school calendars, as well as to appoint teachers
- indigenous peoples' involvement as consultants and teachers, in particular in mother-tongue instruction in early childhood and primary education
- meaningful positions for indigenous representatives in school boards and policy-making committees, as well as in institutions of the state education system, and
- support for the implementation of indigenous peoples' own educational plans, programmes, curricula and materials and the establishment of their own educational institutions to enhance responsibility and ownership of indigenous peoples over educational practices and contents.

II. 2
PEDAGOGY AND METHODOLOGY

Pedagogical concepts are embedded in culture and guided by the specific educational priorities and goals of a given society. They are reflected in models of generating and transmitting knowledge and skills, in teaching methods and learning styles.

The challenge is to accommodate indigenous and non-indigenous concepts that are evolving in a historical and political context. In indigenous education, a balance needs to be made between formal and non-formal, and between traditional and modern teaching methods, guided by the objective of empowering indigenous peoples to be informed and active members of their own communities as well as of the national community.

Education that aims at liberating and empowering indigenous peoples implies a pedagogy that starts from the situation of the indigenous culture itself. This is a process that involves sensitizing and awareness-raising on the part of educators as a basis for strengthening self-esteem and expanding the existing knowledge and skills of the indigenous learners/community, as well as confronting problems and initiating changes to the current situation. [30]

An analysis of the current situation and the identification of learners' and communities' needs is essential for developing a learner- and community-centred pedagogy, situated in the overall context of learners' daily lives and well-being. Such an approach helps to motivate learners, as the acquisition of knowledge imparted in the classroom or other educational settings is linked to the daily practical use of knowledge and skills. The analysis of the current situation should include such factors as health, gender roles, the stability of the home life and the natural environment. [31] It can also include geographical factors such as the location of the nearest schools for formal education, as well as transport and funding for alternative facilities of non-formal education in the absence of formal facilities. This is particularly the case for those indigenous communities located in remote areas.

Unlike formal Western education – where the content and goals of programmes and the teaching methods and time frames for specific curricula are defined by the educational authorities of cities, regions or countries – in indigenous education it is important that indigenous community members, parents and elders are actively involved in determining what their young people should learn. Methods used by parents at home to teach their children how to prepare food or keep house, for example, might be incorporated in the school. Research on learning outside of school could make a significant contribution to teaching methods. [32] Combining traditional practices and knowledge with curriculum subjects in a contextual way strengthens the link between the community and the school and provides the basis for the community's further integral development.

This may be supported by:

- excursions: to learn about the cultural significance of places and their specific flora and fauna as well as associated stories, ceremonies, beliefs, usages, etc.
- participation in ceremonies with family members, to learn about rituals, associated songs, dances, astrological observations etc., and
- the production of artefacts, using local material and techniques, revitalizing and maintaining traditional practices. [33]

Failing to include traditional learning modes in the classroom can create passive learners not in tune with the teaching methods followed in school. Children may fail to identify not only with the content of learning but also with the way in which the learning experience is organized.

The structuring of the physical learning space, such as the arrangements of classrooms or teaching in the natural environment, to respond to and reflect a specific cultural teacher-learner-relation is also crucial. In conventional classroom arrangements, teachers usually stand or sit in front of the students, who are sitting down in rows. However, circles might be arranged, the 'classroom' might be moved to a field or forest, or learning spaces could be structured taking into account a community's cosmological and social order.

Quality indigenous education is guided by pedagogical principles and methods developed in participation with indigenous communities and based on their culture and tradition, where:

- Education is seen as connected to all aspects of life, the well-being of learners and the environment/land
- The situation of indigenous communities is the starting point for developing the potential of learners and communities according to their own views, values, priorities and aspirations
- Indigenous community members, parents and elders are consulted and involved regarding what their students should, and want to, learn – and when and how – as a basis for identifying pedagogical principles and teaching methods at the start of a programme
- Both formal and non-formal, as well as traditional and modern, teaching methods are used, based on the study of traditional teaching methods at home and in the community
- A co-operative, interactive and reflexive learning-teaching process is promoted, based on all aspects of knowledge and the experience of learners.

II. 3
INDIGENOUS KNOWLEDGE

The proper recognition and inclusion of indigenous knowledge in planning and implementing education programmes, policies and curricula is a complex issue [34] that needs to be understood within the given political, cultural and socio-economic contexts. Indigenous knowledge may include scientific, mathematical, medicinal, taxonomic, artistic, environmental, philosophical and other knowledge.

However, indigenous knowledge is not homogenous, and not all knowledge is necessarily shared by everyone in the indigenous community, but rather depends on age, gender and specific roles. In the context of education, *who* holds or 'owns' *what* knowledge is crucial, as well as to whom and by whom this knowledge is transmitted. These questions as well as the social roles and relationships reflected in and affected by modes of holding and transmitting knowledge need to be taken into account in the development of curricula. The support and consent of indigenous communities in identifying which knowledge may be included, and how, is essential. This also applies to copyright authority and rights regarding the documentation of indigenous knowledge and the production of educational material in indigenous languages. [35]

A survey of attitudes regarding the use and inclusion of Navajo language and culture in all schools in the Navajo Nation explains:

> Though many concerns were voiced, respondents were very consistent in agreement that some components of Navajo culture did not belong in schools.

Religious and ceremonial instruction were mentioned time after time as areas that were best left to those outside the school to teach. [36]

Quality indigenous education offers innovative solutions to the complex issue of incorporating indigenous knowledge, and values indigenous-knowledge systems as equal and complementary to Western systems. This includes:

- respect for, and recognition of ownership of, indigenous communities as holders of indigenous knowledge, and for their specific ways of generating and transmitting knowledge
- identification and incorporation of relevant local cultural knowledge with the participation and informed consent of indigenous communities and elders, in particular as regards the selection, transmission and documentation of that knowledge – in the planning of programmes, the selection of teaching methods, the design of curricula and the production of educational material
- inclusion of stories, diaries, textbooks, etc., as well as non-verbal education materials produced by indigenous teachers
- the active participation of students and community members who serve to develop a curriculum founded on indigenous people's cultural identity and history.

II. 4
CURRICULUM

The challenge in indigenous education lies in establishing links between indigenous knowledge and skills and national standard curricula. Based on the recognition of different yet equal and complementary systems of knowledge and world views, making this linkage is a gradual process and may be achieved through:

- placing priority on learning about the indigenous culture in early childhood and primary education, proceeding later to learning about other values and cultures
- providing instruction in the indigenous community's values, traditions, language, and agricultural techniques, while at the same time preparing students with the practical skills they need to participate in the national society
- emphasizing the study of traditional life and culture in formal education systems and advocating curricula that put local heritage on an equal footing with standard subjects such as maths, science and natural history. [37]

Curricula in indigenous education should be place- and community-based and include elements of the local flora and fauna and the development of seasonal-environmental curricula, where appropriate, following the traditional relationship with the land. [38] Botanical knowledge, for example, might best be taught through excursions during seasons when certain plants or herbs are harvested or collected.

Curricula which avoid over-specialization and are connected to the learner's daily life in the community strengthen the identity and learning capacity of the indigenous learner. An example of how various subjects can be addressed in a curriculum unit – integrating traditional knowledge and diverse learning opportunities – is illustrated below, taking 'snow' as a core theme.[39]

Table 1.1

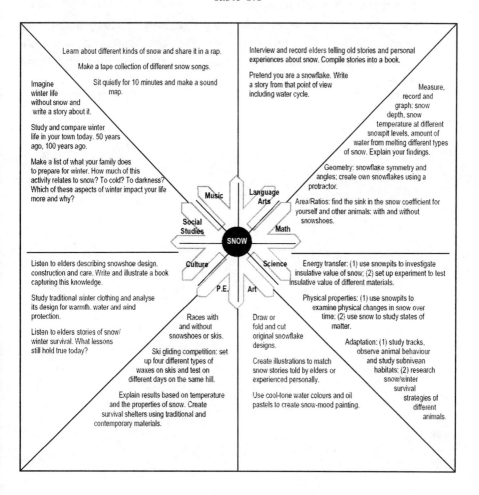

Quality indigenous education means developing curricula that place emphasis on and are connected to indigenous culture, knowledge and language. Such curricula:

- are designed with the active involvement of indigenous communities
- gradually integrate indigenous and Western forms of knowledge and ways of knowing
- are place- and culture-based
- include seasonal-environmental curricula and the use of local flora and fauna
- reflect the interrelation of subjects
- also promote positive attitudes to indigenous languages and cultures among the non-indigenous population, to promote understanding, tolerance and solidarity between different cultural groups.

II. 5
LANGUAGES OF INSTRUCTION

Language is not only a tool for communication and knowledge but also a fundamental attribute of cultural identity and empowerment, both for the individual and the group. [40]

It is crucial to support and promote the survival and the use of indigenous languages in indigenous education as one of the essential elements of indigenous cultures and identities. The knowledge, the specific ways of thinking and of interpreting the world, and the cultural values of a society, community or group are contained and reflected in their language and transmitted inter-generationally through this medium. Language education encompasses not only the teaching and learning *of* language, but also learning *through* language. It opens up other ways of interpreting the world and promotes understanding of other cultures. Intercultural bilingual education is concerned with the promotion of cross-cultural understanding and the respect of cultural and linguistic diversity. UNESCO supports the view that in order to gain a deeper understanding of other cultures, the cultural component of language teaching and learning should be strengthened. It is therefore important to link language and culture in education. [41]

Yet the use of indigenous languages in educational programmes is a complex and even contested issue. In addition to legal questions regarding the status of indigenous languages in relation to official and national languages, it raises such issues as the role and social meaning of literacy, the use and importance of written language, and the cultural role and use of language as a medium of communication and transmission of knowledge. It is crucial to consider cultural values and communities' priorities and choices as regards the language of instruction and the teaching of literacy in indigenous, official and national languages. Learning a second language – as well as learning the knowledge contained in that new language – at the same time as one is learning to read and write places additional demands on a learner.[42]

The use of indigenous languages as both the medium and the subject of instruction needs to take into consideration the linguistic situation of the indigenous community and of the learners, which can be broadly subsumed under two main categories:

a) learners who acquired the indigenous language at home and are either monolingual or dominant in that language, and who will learn the national language as a second language, and

b) learners who are dominant or monolingual in the national language, or who are bilingual, and who will learn the indigenous language as a second language.[43]

Some support the view that:

It makes good educational sense for initial literacy to be taught to young children in their first language, a language they can actually understand, and for second language acquisition ... to take place on the basis of that firm foundation.[44]

This view is supported by UNESCO, which considers mother-tongue instruction as being essential, both in initial instruction and in literacy programmes – for children as well as adults – and underlines that learning of and through a second language should take place in a gradual manner based on the learners' literacy in their mother tongue and their knowledge of the second language as a subject of learning.[45]

Learning of and through the indigenous language may need to go hand in hand with a language revitalization programme when the indigenous group is already proficient in the national language. It may in these cases make more sense for initial instruction and literacy to be in the national language. However, decisions regarding the use of indigenous languages need to be made with the participation of members of the indigenous community: learners, parents and elders, and should also take into account that:

There is a strong consensus between social and educational sciences suggesting that using the mother tongue at school, within the framework of a bilingual maintenance programme, strengthens the student's intellectual and linguistic development, reinforces their identity, and invigorates them to enforce/practice their cultural rights. [46]

Models of intercultural bilingual or multilingual education address the need to balance the use and teaching of the mother tongue with the learning of other languages in a culturally appropriate way. Such models include *additive* approaches to bilingualism, which aim at conserving and improving the mother tongue through instruction in the mother tongue, with the second language being added on at a later stage. In contrast, *subtractive* bilingualism aims to teach first in the mother tongue, and then to move on to the second language after a transition period, at which point the second language becomes the only one used in the classroom. These approaches have different aims and outcomes in terms of proficiency in the mother tongue and in the second language.

Despite the importance of using indigenous languages and the advantages of intercultural bilingual programmes in indigenous education, a number of problems may be encountered, including:

- lack of recognition of indigenous languages, including legal recognition, in comparison to official language(s)
- lack of material, especially written material in indigenous languages
- lack of teachers trained to teach in more than one language
- limited use and a limited number of speakers of the indigenous language(s) in indigenous communities, meaning that students learn their indigenous language as a second language
- rejection of the use of indigenous languages in school by parents because they have experienced discrimination when using their mother tongue and fear that their children will not learn the official language well enough
- existence and use of variants of the indigenous language in addition to the official one
- low proficiency in both the indigenous and the second language due to inadequate methods and lack of cultural embeddedness of programmes
- representation of more than one indigenous language by students in the same class/group, etc. [47]

Approaches to solving these problems include the promotion of language policies that recognize and implement indigenous peoples' linguistic and educational rights; revitalization programmes for indigenous languages; research and registering of indigenous languages in co-operation with elder speakers; the development of alphabets for, and educational material in, indigenous languages, by students and teachers, as part of the process of instruction in the mother tongue; capacity building of teachers; the involvement of native speakers as (co-)teachers; and instruction in groups arranged according to their mother tongue.[48]

As it is advocated that indigenous languages are the best way to teach indigenous knowledge and values, it is also important to support the creation of, and reflection on the context of, written material and curricula based on indigenous knowledge and in indigenous languages.[49]

Quality indigenous education supports the use of indigenous languages while encouraging fluency in the national language and access to wide international languages by:

- Recognizing that language is not only a tool for communication and knowledge but also a fundamental element of cultural identity
- Teaching and learning indigenous knowledge and curricula through indigenous language and the use of locally researched and produced material in indigenous languages
- Teaching and learning of and through the mother tongue in early schooling and literacy instruction, and moving on to learning other languages in a culturally appropriate and gradual way, according to learners' capacities and needs
- Involving native speakers of indigenous languages as teachers
- Learning other languages as a basis for cross-cultural understanding and tolerance.

II. 6
TEACHER TRAINING

Quality indigenous education also depends on the teachers. Bilingual teachers need to be trained to teach in more than one language and culture. Unfortunately, it is not always the case that they are. Their training should include specific components concerning bilingual students and inter-cultural classrooms, as well as specific methodologies for language training. Ability to speak the indigenous language as well as the official one is vital for teachers in indigenous education. Teachers in indigenous schools face a special challenge in terms of learning about, creating and applying teaching methods that respond to the specific learning styles and needs of indigenous communities. Methods need to be continuously assessed, evaluated and redefined with the participation of students, their parents and communities. This also requires teachers to engage in a continuous training process to enable them to use and develop appropriate teaching methods. Unfortunately, such training is not always available.

As was pointed out above, indigenous elders need to be recognized, respected and involved as teachers, a goal that can be facilitated through 'Elders-in-Residence' programmes, for example. [50] Often teachers in indigenous education need to create and develop their own teaching materials together with the indigenous communities, simply because these are not otherwise available.

Quality indigenous education involves competent and qualified teachers who are:

- familiar with indigenous culture and language as well as the national culture and language
- respectful to indigenous concepts and values regarding education, and who engage in an interactive process with indigenous communities and students
- using and creating responsive and experiential teaching methods and material in co-operation and consultation with the indigenous community
- trained in bilingual teaching methods and language-training methodologies
- open to continuous assessment of their work and teaching practices
- trained in teacher-training programmes and facilities organized in cooperation with indigenous peoples' organizations and communities
- selected in consultation with indigenous communities.

II. 7
MATERIALS

Educational materials need to be learner-centred. This includes the use of material in the mother tongue, incorporating the oral tradition of the communities into the learning materials, as well as audio-visual and graphic material. [51]

The following experience of a teacher who, though native, was of a different cultural origin than her students, illustrates the importance of relating educational material to the daily reality, world view and interpretation of the learners:

> I set up a pretty little fishing pond with beautiful blue cardboard for water so the construction paper fish could 'swim' in it. When you fished with the pole, the magnet on the end of the string would catch the fish. There were many colors because this was a bilingual color-learning game. I was proud; the kids would love it. Early that morning, Alfonso and Morris were the first students in the room. They ran over to see what was new in the corner. They kept pointing and talking to each other in Keres [their indigenous language]. I encouraged them to fish for colors, showing them how. They still seemed hesitant. They pointed to the cardboard (water) and said in a rather dissatisfied tone, 'Not blue, brown'. How many times had I crossed the bridge over the Rio Grande and seen the water – but not 'seen' the water? It was brown, not blue (Skinner, 1999, p. 110).

Mother-tongue instruction often requires material in indigenous languages that is not always available and consequently has to be developed by teachers and students.

Such material may involve:

- oral content: narratives, stories, myths, and the use of audio tapes
- visual media: videos, films, maps
- paintings, sculpture and music, as well as performance
- ICTs and Internet
- flora and fauna.

Quality indigenous education makes use of and produces innovative and culturally adequate teaching material based on indigenous and Western educational concepts, including:

- material based on respect for the cultural values and specific relationship with nature of indigenous communities
- visual, sensual and practical materials for non-verbal communication
- material in indigenous languages and incorporating indigenous knowledge produced with the participation and consent of indigenous communities, teachers and learners
- material that promotes an interactive learning – teaching process
- material that provides an accurate picture and fair information on indigenous cultures and ways of life.

II. 8
ASSESSMENT AND EVALUATION

Assessment and evaluation are essential to ensure the quality of educational programmes and to meet the learning needs of students. In indigenous education, assessment and evaluation are guided by the objective of enabling and empowering students to become culturally grounded and knowledgeable participants and actors in their own communities as well as in the national and global society. This means basing assessment and evaluation on culturally appropriate standards and criteria as well as on general national standards. Characteristics of multiple assessment and evaluation strategies include:

*   assessment and evaluation as the responsibility of parents, elders, teachers, communities and schools
*   assessment and evaluation as integral parts of instruction
*   assessment and evaluation as informal everyday events
*   assessment and evaluation as a continuous process. [52]

Assessment and evaluation, understood as a continuous and collaborative process in learning and teaching, are not limited to testing students' performance at the end of a programme or school-term, but rather include such strategies as observation, informal interviews, self-evaluation and continual assessment of performance throughout the programme or term. It may involve the following actors:

- Elders and community
- Parents
- Teachers
- Students
- School boards and educational authorities
- Researchers.

These should support the integration of traditional indigenous strategies with standardized strategies, such as inquiry and testing in assessment and evaluation, in order to identify educational development in terms of cultural knowledge and skills, including proficiency in local and national languages, as well as academic and scientific knowledge.

However, assessment and evaluation not only concern the learning outcomes of students – their performance, knowledge, skills, values and attitudes, but also:

- teaching methods and practices
- teachers' performance
- curriculum
- materials, and
- the programme as a whole.

Table 1.2 provides suggestions regarding the integration of traditional and inquiry assessment strategies in culturally responsive science instruction. [53]

In applying multiple culturally appropriate and nationally recognized strategies in assessment and evaluation, participants can contribute to the growth of culturally knowledgeable students who are well grounded in, and support, their indigenous culture and community, and who are at the same time able to participate in a variety of cultural environments and to achieve personal and academic success in significant and measurable terms, including according to national education standards. [54]

While the following synthesized criteria regarding assessment and evaluation try to provide further guidance, care needs to be taken that the respect for the right to be different of indigenous peoples does not lead to the creation of a kind of second-class education for indigenous peoples. Therefore, it is important to create and apply assessment strategies and

Table 1.2

Traditional Assessment	Inquiry Assessment	Compatible Assessment Strategies
1. *Diagnostic*		
• Standards are set using cultural knowledge continuum and 'need to know' as a guide • Watching and interacting with children in daily life and gauging individual readiness for specific tasks	• Standards and district curriculum used as guide to instructional priorities • Prior to instruction, student's background experiences, skills, attitudes and misconceptions are gauged	• Informal discussions of topic to be studied • Observational evidence from prior activities • Concept mapping
2. *Formative*		
• Observing children at work on task during daily life, offering continued modelling, encouragement and positive acknowledgments of individual progress • Provision of additional tasks as students' skills and knowledge develop and they appear ready for the next challenge • Skills and knowledge are not assessed in isolation from their purpose and application	• Monitoring student progress and adjusting learning activities to reach goals • Provision of helpful feedback to improve student's understanding • Assessments tap developing skills, attitudes and conceptual understanding	• Observations • Informal interviews • Journals and learning logs • Self-evaluations • Performance tasks
3. *Summative*		
• Ultimate evaluation is whether or not child can apply learning effectively in daily life (e.g. do they have adequate skills and understanding to successfully trap hares, collect and preserve berries, etc.)	• Assessment of student's ability to transfer skills and understanding to other tasks in other contexts	• Performance tasks • Performance events • Self-evaluations • Portfolios • Creative performances and exhibitions

standards that respond to indigenous peoples' culture, needs and goals, without imposing a different and perhaps simplistic and inefficient 'indigenous normative system'. [55]

Quality indigenous education uses multiple assessment strategies involving elders, parents and learners, teachers, researchers, and school leaders in a collaborative process to assess and evaluate:

- Learning outcomes (in terms of students' cultural knowledge, practical skills and understanding, and their ability to use these in different contexts): through observation, practical assessment, linking students' performance at home with that in schools, as well as through standardized and norm-based tests, when and where appropriate
- Teaching methods and practices (in terms of cultural responsiveness and effectiveness in promoting student growth, vis-à-vis the national curriculum): through self-assessment and participatory research by educators, observation and review by elders and parents, as well as through interviewing students and comparing their learning activities at home and in school
- Teachers' performance (in terms of their ability to utilize different instruction strategies and to provide multiple learning opportunities for students, as well as their competence in regard local and national languages, and their cultural knowledge): through self-assessment and participatory research by teachers themselves, through the involvement of indigenous communities in selecting, advising and assessing teachers, and through the provision of opportunities for teachers to expand their cultural knowledge and pedagogical skills
- Curriculum (in terms of content, priorities, timing and the interrelation of subjects, based on national as well as cultural standards): through continuous review and redefinition by all educational actors
- Materials (in terms of their accuracy and appropriateness, in relation to the local cultural context and natural environment): through the establishing of review committees, and using multiple levels and perspectives in the creation and review of textbooks and other curriculum materials
- Programmes as a whole (in terms of the incorporation of indigenous culture and language): through meetings, committees and informal events to plan, review and redefine programmes. [56]

NOTES FOR PARTS I AND II:

1. According to ILO Convention No. 169, indigenous people are descendants of those populations that inhabited a country or geographical region at the time of conquest or colonization, when people of different cultures or ethnic origins arrived and became dominant. ILO Convention on Indigenous and Tribal Peoples in Independent Countries, 1989 (No. 169), Article 1.1 b). See also UN Fact Sheet No. 9, p. 3.
2. United Nations, 1997, *The Rights of Indigenous Peoples*. Human Rights Fact Sheet No. 9, p. 3.
3. A.T. Durning, 1992, *Guardians of the Land: Indigenous Peoples and the Health of the Earth*. Washington, DC, Worldwatch Institute, Worldwatch Paper no. 112.
4. *World Conference on Human Rights: The Vienna Declaration and Programme of Action*, June 1993. Section II, paragraph 32. The International Decade was proclaimed by the UN General Assembly in its resolution A/RES/48/163 of 18 February 1994.
5. UN General Assembly resolution 50/157 of 21 December 1995, annex, paragraph 1.
6. The UN Permanent Forum on Indigenous Issues was established in 2000 through the Economic and Social Council resolution 2000/22. The second session was held from 12 to 23 May 2003 in New York. See report of the Second Session E/2003/43, E/C.19/2003/22, p. 19, as well as the Mission Report on the Education Meeting by Katherine Grigsby, Chief Technical Advisor, PROMEM, UNESCO Guatemala.
7. UNESCO, 2000, *The Dakar Framework for Action*, p. 12.
8. UN General Assembly resolution 50/157 of 21 December 1995, annex, paragraphs 3 and 4.
9. The Coolangatta Statement on Indigenous Peoples' Rights in Education (1999).
10. These instruments and declarations include: Convention against Discrimination in Education (1960); Convention on the Rights of the Child (1989); ILO Convention 169 on Indigenous and Tribal Peoples in Independent Countries (1989); the Coolangatta Statement on Indigenous Peoples' Rights in Education (1999); the Draft United Nations Declaration on the Rights of Indigenous Peoples (1994); the Hamburg Declaration on Adult Learning (1997); the UNESCO Universal Declaration on Cultural Diversity (2001); and the Lima Declaration on Multilingual Reality and Intercultural Challenge: Citizenship, politics and education 2002.
11. World Declaration on Education for All: Meeting Basic Learning Needs. Adopted by the World Conference on Education for All, Jomtien, Thailand, 5 – 9 March 1990, (preamble, UNESCO, 2000, The Dakar Framework for Action. Education for All: Meeting our Collective Commitments. Adopted by the World Education Forum, Dakar, Senegal, 26 28 April 2000, p. 8.
12. Statement on Indigenous Education Rights by the Committee on Indigenous Education at the Indigenous Preparatory Meeting for the United Nations Working Group on Indigenous Populations, 25 July 1998.

13. CEPAL, 2000, p. 314.

14. Native American Languages Act. PL 104-477. United States Congress. Washington, DC: 30 October 1990. Indigenous Peoples Rights Act, also known as Republic Act (RA) 8371, Philippines (1997), Section 27 & 28. Ley de Educación, Ecuador (1999). Policy called 'Pupil's own language', Malaysia (1997) referred to in: ILO, 2000: ILO Convention on Indigenous and Tribal Peoples, 1989 [No. 169]: a manual, p. 63.

15. See ILO Convention 169, Article 27.3., the UN Draft Declaration on the Rights of Indigenous Peoples, Article 15, the Proposed American Declaration on the Rights of Indigenous Peoples (Approved by the Inter-American Commission on Human Rights, 1997) Article IX.1.

16. Status Report on Indigenous Education in Australia and Aotearoa/New Zealand, 1995, p. 5.

17. See for example Bin-Sallik and Smibert, 1998.

18. UNESCO, 2000: The Dakar Framework for Action. Expanded Commentary, p. 13.

19. See Lopez, 1998; and The Coolangatta Statement on Indigenous Peoples' Rights in Education (1999).

20. Proceedings of the First Hemispheric Conference on Indigenous Education, Guatemala, 25 – 27 July 2001: Part II, Synthesis in English, p. 7 ff.

21. UNESCO Education Position Paper: Education in a Multilingual World, 2003, p. 33.

22. Proceedings of the First Hemispheric Conference on Indigenous Education, Guatemala, 25 – 27 July 2001: Part II, Synthesis in English, p. 19 and Cunningham, 2001, Part III, p. 2.

23. Lima Declaration on Multilingual Reality and Intercultural Challenge: Citizenship, politics and education. Result of the V Congress on Intercultural Bilingual Education held in Lima, 6 – 9 August 2002.

24. See Proceedings of the First Hemispheric Conference on Indigenous Education, Guatemala, 25 – 27 July 2001: Part II, Synthesis in English, p. 12 and Richards and Blanchet-Cohen, 2000, p. 22.

25. See Richards and Blanchet-Cohen, 2000; Tippeconnic III, 1999; Lopez, 1998; Bin-Sallik and Smibert, 1998; as well as ILO, 2000: ILO Convention on Indigenous and Tribal Peoples, 1989 [No. 169]: a manual, p. 66.

26. See Article 4 and 5 and Objective 14 of the UNESCO Universal Declaration on Cultural Diversity.

27. UNESCO, 2000: The Dakar Framework for Action. Expanded Commentary, p. 17.

28. See Stiles, 1997. Note: It has to be taken into account though that the indigenous language is not necessarily spoken at home in indigenous communities and that often parents start revaluing and relearning their mother tongue in the course of bilingual primary education of their children.

29. Alaska Native Knowledge Network, 2000, p. 26.

30. See Zúñiga, 1999, p. 50; and Freire, 1971.

31. UNESCO, 1999: Manual on Functional Literacy for Indigenous Peoples, pp. 6–7 and 25. UNESCO Principal Regional Office for Asia and the Pacific. Bangkok.
UNESCO, 2003: Draft Manual on Minority Language Communities in Asia. Chapter 3, p. 1. UNESCO Principal Regional Office for Asia and the Pacific. Bangkok.

32. See Nagai, 2000; and Lipka, 2002.

33. Lopes da Silva, 1999, p. 263.

34. King, 1999, p. 249.

35. Alaska Native Knowledge Network, 2000, p. 4.

36. Batchelder, A. and Markel, S., 1997.

37. Ashoka Fellow Profiles: Mexico and Thailand. Retrieved on 26 October 2002 from Ashoka website: www.ashoka.org/global/education.cfm, Hernandez, 2001, p. 32.

38. See Skinner, 1999; and Jacobs and Reyhner, 2002.

39. The diagram has been reproduced from Stephens, Sidney: Handbook for Culturally Responsive Science Curriculum, p. 33.

40. UNESCO Education Position Paper: Education in a Multilingual World, 2003, p. 16.

41. UNESCO Education Position Paper: Education in a Multilingual World, 2003, p. 33.

42. UNESCO Education Position Paper: Education in a Multilingual World, 2003, p. 13; and UNESCO, 1999: Manual on Functional Literacy for Indigenous Peoples, p. 55.

43. Francis, N. and Reyhner, J., 2002, p. 10.

44. Christine Nicholls, 2000. This is also supported by Lopez, Wright et al and others.

45. UNESCO Position Paper: Education in a Multilingual World, 2003, p. 31.

46. Duque, 1998, p. 73. Supported by, for example: Wright, S. C.; Taylor, D. M.; Ruggeiro, K. M.; MacArthur, J.; and Elijassiapik, M. (1996).

47. See UNESCO Position Paper; and Duque, 1998.

48. See Stiles, 1997; and UNESCO Position Paper, p. 31.

49. The Coolangatta Statement, 1999.

50. See Nagai, 2000; and Skinner, 1999.

51. UNESCO, 1999: Manual on Functional Literacy for Indigenous Peoples. p. 42.

52. Nagai, 2000, p. 10.

53. This table is adapted from Stephens, S.: Handbook for Culturally Responsive Science Curriculum, p. 35.

54. ANKN, 1998, p. 5 and 6; Lipka, 2002.

55. Lopes da Silva, 1999, p. 265.

56. ANKN, 1998, p. 20; ANKN, 1999, p. 12–16; ANKN, 2000, p. 9–14.

REFERENCES FOR PARTS I AND II

CONVENTIONS AND DECLARATIONS:

Convention against Discrimination in Education (1960).

Convention on the Rights of the Child (1989).

ILO Convention 169 on Indigenous and Tribal Peoples in Independent Countries (1989).

Draft United Nations Declaration on the Rights of Indigenous Peoples (1994).

Proposed American Declaration on the Rights of Indigenous Peoples (text as approved by the Inter-American Commission on Human Rights in 1997).

The Hamburg Declaration on Adult Learning (1997). Adopted at the Fifth International Conference on Adult Education, CONFINTEA V, held by UNESCO in Hamburg, 14 – 18 July 1997.

The Coolangatta Statement on Indigenous Peoples' Rights in Education (1999). Ratified during the World Indigenous Peoples Conference on Education held in Hilo, Hawaii, in 1999. Retrieved from: http://www.fnahec.org/wipce2002/coolongatta/coolongotta_text.html.

The UNESCO Universal Declaration on Cultural Diversity (2001).

The Lima Declaration on Multilingual Reality and Intercultural Challenge: Citizenship, politics and education. Result of the V Congress on Intercultural Bilingual Education held in Lima, 6 – 9 August 2002.

World Declaration on Education for All: Meeting Basic Learning Needs. Adopted by the World Conference on Education for All, Jomtien, Thailand, 5 – 9 March 1990.

United Nations World Conference on Human Rights: The Vienna Declaration and Programme of Action, June 1993.

REFERENCES:

Alaska Native Knowledge Network. 1998. *Alaska Standards for Culturally Responsive Schools.* Retrieved from: http://www.ankn.uaf.edu.
——. 1999. *Guidelines Preparing Culturally Responsive Teachers for Alaska's Schools.* Retrieved from: http://www.ankn.uaf.edu.
——. 2000. *Guidelines for Respecting Cultural Knowledge.* Retrieved from: http://www.ankn.uaf.edu.
Ashoka. *Ashoka Fellow Profiles: Mexico and Thailand.* Retrieved from Ashoka website: http://www.ashoka.org/global/education.cfm on 26 October 2002.
Bastias, U. 1999. The Education Dimension in Projects with Women. In: I. Jung and L. King (ed.), *Gender, Innovation and Education in Latin America.* UNESCO Institute for Education and Deutsche Stiftung für internationale Entwicklung (DSE).
Batchelder, A. and Markel, S. 1997. An Initial Exploration of the Navajo Nation's Language and Culture Initiative. In: Jon Reyhner (ed.) *Teaching Indigenous Languages.* Flagstaff, Ariz.: Northern Arizona University, pp. 239–47.
Bin-Sallik, M. A. and Smibert, N. 1998. Anangu Teacher Education: An integrated adult education programme. In: L. King (ed) *Reflecting Visions: New Perspectives on Adult Education for Indigenous Peoples.* UNESCO Institute for Education/University of Waikato.
Burger, J. 1998. Indigenous Peoples: Progress in the International Recognition of Human Rights and the Role of Education. In: L. King (ed) *Reflecting Visions: New Perspectives on Adult Education for Indigenous Peoples.* UNESCO Institute for Education/University of Waikato.
Cantoni, G. (ed.). 1996. *Stabilizing Indigenous Languages.* Flagstaff Ariz.: Center for

Excellence in Education, Northern Arizona University. Retrieved from http://jan.ucc.nau.edu/~jar/LIB/LIBconts.

CEPAL 2000. *Equidad, desarrollo y cuidadanía*. United Nations/CEPAL.

Classen, C. 1999. Other Ways to Wisdom: Learning through the Senses across Cultures. In: L. King (ed.) *Learning, Knowledge and Cultural Context*. Kluwer Academic Publishers (UNESCO Institute for Education).

Cunningham, M. 2001. Educación Intercultural Bilingüe en los Contextos Multiculturales. In: *Proceedings of the First Hemispheric Conference on Indigenous Education*. Guatemala, 25 – 27 July 2001: Part III.

Duque, V. 1998. The Educational Reality of the Indigenous Peoples of the Mesoamerican Region. In: L. King (ed.) *Reflecting Visions: New Perspectives on Adult Education for Indigenous Peoples*. UNESCO Institute for Education/The University of Waikato.

Durning, A.T. 1992. *Guardians of the Land: Indigenous Peoples and the Health of the Earth*. Washington, DC Worldwatch Institute. Worldwatch Paper no. 112. Referred to in: G.T. Oviedo; A. Gonzales and L. Maffi (2001) *The Importance of and Ways to Conserve and Protect Traditional Ecological Knowledge*. WWF and Terralingua.

Emery, A.R. 2000. *Guidelines: Integrating Indigenous Knowledge in Project Planning and Implementation*. A Partnership Publication: The International Labour Organization, The World Bank, The Canadian International Development Agency, and KIVU Nature Inc. Retrieved from The World Bank's website: http://www.worldbank.org.

Fantani, A. 2001. Conceptos, Contextos y Modelos de la Educación Bilingüe-Intercultural. In: *Proceedings of the First Hemispheric Conference on Indigenous Education*. Guatemala, 25 – 27 July 2001, Part V.

Francis, N. and Reyhner, J. 2002. *Language and Literacy Teaching for Indigenous Education: A Bilingual Approach*. Multilingual Matters.

Freire, P. 1971. *Pedagogy of the Oppressed*.

Gleich von, U. 1998. Linguistic Rights and the Role of Indigenous Languages in Adult Education. In: L. King (ed.) *Reflecting Visions: New Perspectives on Adult Education for Indigenous Peoples*. UNESCO Institute for Education and The University of Waikato.

Gorjestani, N. 2000. *Indigenous Knowledge for Development: Opportunities and Challenges*. The World Bank, Africa Region, The World Bank. This paper is based on a presentation made by the author, who is Chief Knowledge Officer, at the UNCTAD Conference on Traditional Knowledge in Geneva, 1 November 2000. The paper was completed after the Conference and includes some additional material, which has since become available. Retrieved from the World Bank's website: http://www.worldbank.org.

Hernandez, N. 2001. De la Educación Indígena a la Educación Entercultural. La Experiencia de México: Un Breve Repaso. In: *Proceedings of the First Hemispheric Conference on Indigenous Education*, Guatemala, 25–27 July: Part III.

Hopenhayn, M. and Bello, A. 2001. Discriminación étnico-racial y xenofobia en América Latina y el Caribe. CEPAL.

Jacobs, D.T. and Reyhner, J. 2002. *Preparing Teachers to Support American Indian and Alaska Native Student Success and Cultural Heritage*. ERIC Digest EDO-RC-01-13 (January 2002). Retrieved from: http://www.indianeduresearch.net/edorc01-13.htm.

ILO. 2000. ILO Convention on Indigenous and Tribal Peoples, 1989 [No. 169]: a manual. International Labour Organization, Geneva.

Indigenous Peoples Rights Act, also known as Republic Act (RA) 8371. 1997. Philippines.

I. Jung and L. King (ed.). 1999. *Gender, Innovation and Education in Latin America*. UNESCO Institute for Education and Deutsche Stiftung für internationale Entwicklung (DSE).

King, L. 1999. Editorial Introduction to L. King (ed.) *Learning, Knowledge and Cultural Context*. Kluwer Academic Publishers (UNESCO Institute for Education).

——. (ed.). 1999. *Learning, Knowledge and Cultural Context*. Kluwer Academic Publishers (UNESCO Institute for Education).

——. 1998. *Reflecting Visions: New Perspectives on Adult Education for Indigenous Peoples*. UNESCO Institute for Education and The University of Waikato.

Knight, K. 1998. Inuit Experiences in Education and Training Projects. In: L. King (ed.) *Reflecting Visions: New Perspectives on Adult Education for Indigenous Peoples*. UNESCO Institute for Education and The University of Waikato.

Lewis, M.P. 2001. Métodos Pedagógicos Bilingües-Biculturales en el area K'iche. In: *Proceedings of the First Hemispheric Conference on Indigenous Education*. Guatemala, 25 – 27 July. Part IV.

Ley de Educación. 1999. Ecuador.

Lipka, J. 2002. *Schooling for Self-Determination: Research on the Effects of Including Native Language and Culture in the Schools*. ERIC Digest EDO-RC-01-12, January. Retrieved from http://www.indianeduresearch.net/edorc01-12.htm.

Lopes da Silva, A. 1999. Enfants autochtones et apprentissage: La corporalité comme langage en Amérique du Sud tropicale. In: L. King (ed.) *Learning, Knowledge and Cultural Context*. Kluwer Academic Publishers (UNESCO Institute for Education).

Lopez, L.E. 1998. Capacity Building: Lessons Learnt from the Literacy Campaign of the Assembly of the Guarani People of Bolivia. In: L. King (ed.) *Reflecting Visions: New Perspectives on Adult Education for Indigenous Peoples*. UNESCO Institute for Education and The University of Waikato.

Nagai, Y. 2000. *Developing a culturally more appropriate elementary school: An example of Participatory Action Research (PAR) In Papua New Guinea*. A paper presented at ASA Conference, London, 2 – 5 April. Retrieved from: http://www.asa.anthropology.ac.uk/ASA2000.html.

Native American Languages Act. PL 104-477. United States Congress. Washington, DC: October 30, 1990. In: G. Cantoni (ed.) *Stabilizing Indigenous Languages*. Flagstaff:

Center for Excellence in Education, Northern Arizona University. Retrieved from: http://jan.ucc.nau.edu/~jar/LIB/LIBconts.

Nicholls, C. 2000. The Closure of the Bilingual Education Programs in Australia's Northern Territory – What is at Stake? A Former School Principal's Perspective. Copyright ICP & Cyber Text. Retrieved from: www.icponline.org/feature_articles/f18_01.htm.

Proceedings of the First Hemispheric Conference on Indigenous Education, Guatemala, 25 – 27 July 2001. Retrieved from: http://www.worldlearning.org/feria.

Rameka, N. 1998. Tiaki Nga Taonga Nga Tupuna: Valuing the Treasures. In: L. King (ed.) *Reflecting Visions: New Perspectives on Adult Education for Indigenous Peoples.* 1998. UNESCO Institute for Education and The University of Waikato.

Reyhner, J. (ed.) 1997. *Teaching Indigenous Languages.* Flagstaff, AZ: Northern Arizona University. Retrieved from: http://jan.ucc.nau.edu/~jar/TIL.html.

Richards, C. and Blanchet-Cohen, N. 2000. Adult Education and Indigenous Peoples in Canada. In: *International Survey on Adult Education for Indigenous Peoples.* UNESCO Institute for Education. Retrieved from http://www.unesco.org/education/uie/survey/survey.htm.

Skinner, L. 1999. Teaching Through Traditions: Incorporating languages and culture into curricula. In: K. G. Swisher and J. W. Tippeconnic III (eds.) *Next steps: Research and practice to advance Indian education.* Charleston, WV: ERIC/CRESS, pp. 107 34. (ERIC Document Reproduction Service No. ED427907.)

Starkey, H. 2002. *Active Citizenship and the Lifelong Learning Agenda.* Paper presented at the Danish EU Presidency Conference: 'Lifelong Learning – Learning for Adults in the 21st Century', held at Comwell Helsingør, Snekkersten, 7 – 9 October.

Statement on Indigenous Education Rights by the Committee on Indigenous Education at the Indigenous Preparatory Meeting for the United Nations Working Group on Indigenous Populations, 25 July 1998.

Status Report on Indigenous Education in Australia and Aotearoa/New Zealand to Education International Congress, 17 – 22 July 1995, Prepared by: Aboriginal and Torres Strait Islander Members of the Australian Education Union and Maori Members of the New Zealand Education Institute Te Riu Roa, 30 June 1995, quoted in: Education International 1998. *The Status of Indigenous Education: an Overview.* Retrieved from: http://www.ei-ie.org/action/english/etridgrep98.pdf.

Stephens, Sidney 2000. *Handbook for Culturally Responsive Science Curriculum.* Alaska Science Consortium and the Alaska Rural Systemic Initiative. Retrieved from: http://www.ankn.uaf.edu.

Stiles, D.B. 1997. Four Successful Indigenous Language Programs. In: Jon Reyhner (ed.) *Teaching Indigenous Languages,* Flagstaff, AZ: Northern Arizona University, pp. 148–262.

Swisher, K. G and Tippeconnic III, J. W. 1999. *Next steps: Research and practice to advance Indian education.* Charleston, WV: ERIC/CRESS. (ERIC Document Reproduction

Service No. ED427902). Retrieved from: http://www.indianeduresearch.net/edorc01-12.htm.

Tippeconnic III, J. W. 1999. Tribal Control of American Indian Education: Observations since the 1960s with implications for the future. In K. G. Swisher and J. W. Tippeconnic III (eds.) *Next steps: Research and practice to advance Indian education* Charleston, WV: ERIC/CRESS, pp. 33–52. (ERIC Document Reproduction Service No. ED427904.)

Tzay Bajan, C. J. 2001. Currículo Preescolar desde la Cultura y Cosmovisión Maya. In: *Proceedings of the First Hemispheric Conference on Indigenous Education*, Guatemala, 25 – 27 July, Part V.

UNESCO, 1996. *Our Creative Diversity: Report of the World Commission on Culture and Development*.

——. 1999a. *Manual on Functional Literacy for Indigenous Peoples*. UNESCO Principal Regional Office for Asia and the Pacific, Bangkok.

——. 1999b. General Conference Resolution 12: Implementation of a language policy for the world based on multilingualism.

——. 2000. *The Dakar Framework for Action. Education for All: Meeting our Collective Commitments*.

——. 2002. LINKS – Local and Indigenous Knowledge Systems – Project Leaflet.

——. 2003. Education Position Paper: *Education in a Multilingual World*.

——. Forthcoming. Draft Manual on Minority Language Communities in Asia. UNESCO Principal Regional Office for Asia and the Pacific. Bangkok..

United Nations General Assembly resolution 50/157 of 21 December 1995

United Nations 1997. *The Rights of Indigenous Peoples*. Human Rights Fact Sheet No.9.

United Nations Economic and Social Council Resolution 2000/22.

United Nations Economic and Social Council: Permanent Forum on Indigenous Issues, Report on the second session. E/2003/43, E/C.19/2003/22.

Valiente Catter, T. 1998. Youth and Adult Education and Literacy for Indigenous Peoples in Latin America. In L. King (ed.) *Reflecting Visions: New Perspectives on Adult Education for Indigenous Peoples*. UNESCO Institute for Education and The University of Waikato.

Wright, S. C.; Taylor, D. M.; Ruggeiro, K. M.; MacArthur, J.; Elijassiapik, M. 1996. *The Jaanimmarik School Language Testing Project*. Montreal, Quebec: Kativik School Board. Retrieved from: http://www.kativik.qc.ca/downloads/KSBIR_e.pdf.

Zúñiga, M. 1999. Towards a Pedagogy of Education Programmes for Grassroots Women. In: I. Jung and L. King (ed.) *Gender, Innovation and Education in Latin America*. UNESCO Institute for Education and Deutsche Stiftung für internationale Entwicklung (DSE).

PART III. CASE STUDIES CONCERNING THE PROVISION OF QUALITY EDUCATION FOR INDIGENOUS PEOPLES

Part III presents case studies of programmes and initiatives of quality education from different regions of the world where indigenous peoples live. These case studies represent a selection of the wide range of existing institutions, programmes and initiatives and include experiences developed and implemented by indigenous communities and organizations themselves, as well as experiences and programmes supported and implemented by non-governmental organizations and/or governmental institutions in co-operation with indigenous peoples.

This selection is based on the set of criteria elaborated in Part II, with a view to documenting some of the most innovative and successful experiences which could serve as references for actors in the field of indigenous education. The experiences range from early childhood care and education to primary and secondary schools, adult education and teacher training. While not all of the case studies necessarily meet all of the criteria outlined above, and while the individual case studies are not all equally strong regarding each element of the criteria, they do however all represent experiences that have approached the challenge of providing quality education for indigenous peoples in an innovative, participatory and culturally responsive and contextual manner, thereby offering viable and inspiring examples. As the intention in documenting these case studies is not to present perfect models to be copied, problems that might have been encountered in developing the different experiences, and the solutions to these problems, have also been described.

It has not been possible to include case studies from all the regions where indigenous peoples live. One reason for this, and a rather significant one in the context of the subject of the present publication, has to do with the objective of obtaining case studies from people who are actively involved in the respective programmes, and preferably from the indigenous actors involved. However, where indigenous experts are involved at the level of decision-making and implementation of education programmes they are often underrepresented and therefore overburdened with responsibilities, and, consequently, they lack the time to elaborate case studies or similar documents about their experiences.

The following case studies have therefore been elaborated by indigenous experts directly involved in the programmes and/or by advisors and supporters of the programmes, often from non-governmental organizations. Some of the case studies are based on material received from those involved in the experiences, supplemented by other material retrieved from the Internet and revised by the responsible/respective educational actors.

The case studies are presented according to the following structure:

- Type of programme and educational level
- Geographic and administrative aspects
- Indigenous target group(s)
- Description of programme/institution
  - Summary
  - Background: legal-political, socio-economic, educational and linguistic situation
  - Objectives and focus
  - Participation
  - Methods used
  - Language(s) of instruction
  - Curriculum/Themes
  - Teachers/Training
  - Materials and activities
  - Outcomes
- Lessons learnt: strengths and weaknesses
- Duration
- Funding/Budget
- Responsible organization(s)
- Contact

BOTSWANA: THE BOKAMOSO PRE-SCHOOL PROGRAMME[1]

Letloa and Bokamoso Programme

In-service teacher training for early childhood care and education

Type of programme and educational level

Gantsi district, Central Kalahari Reserve, Botswana; San initiative supported by Letloa, the service organization for the Kuru Family of Organizations (KFO) and Working Group of Indigenous Peoples in Southern Africa (WIMSA)

Geographic and administrative aspects

San children and adults (mostly of the Naro language group) in thirteen settlements/communities in the district

Indigenous target group(s)

The Bokamoso Pre-school Programme currently operates in several villages and settlements in the Gantsi District of western Botswana. Bokamoso (which means 'for the future' in Setswana, the national language of Botswana) is the only pre-school teacher-training programme in the region with San trainers. The training programme, begun in 1989, is a two-year in-service course for village teachers who have been selected by their communities.

There are thirteen pre-schools in the villages and settlements in the Gantsi district, two playgroups and a

Description of programme/institution

Summary

pre-school in the Gantsi township, and three playgroups on the farms. This makes altogether in the Gantsi district nineteen early-childhood projects, of which thirteen are centre-based and have a building, a cooking area and outdoor equipment, which parents have erected for their children. The informal playgroups operate outside with a sink house mainly used as a storeroom for materials. The centres have an average of about fifty pupils while the playgroups on the farms and in the township have around twenty to thirty children registered.

Bokamoso is one of eight members of the present Kuru Family of Organizations (KFO). The Kuru Family of Organizations developed out of the Kuru Development Trust, the first NGO in Botswana devoted to a strategy of affirmative action towards the San people and to empowering the San through a holistic approach to development (see KFO webpage).

Even though the focus of the Bokamoso Programme is on pre-school teachers' training, the programme also tries to address the problems that prevent San children from being successful in formal education. Therefore, a number of other training activities target the environment around the San child, such as parent training, orientation for primary-school teachers, etc. Bokamoso works in close co-operation with a Naro literacy project and with other members of the Kuru Family, who provide vocational skills and training to support community members and facilitate their participation in their own development programmes (WIMSA, p. 7).

KFO receives logistical and technical support from Letloa, the partner organization of the South African San Institute (SASI) and the Working Group of Indigenous Minorities in Southern Africa (WIMSA), a regional networking organization for San organizations in southern Africa. WIMSA also co-ordinates a programme supporting activities on Education, Culture and Language among the San organizations in southern Africa. The Bokamoso Programme is a longstanding partner of the Bernard Van Leer Foundation, which funds this regional programme (WIMSA, p. 7).

The San (or Basarwa, or Bushmen) are one of the oldest indigenous populations of the world, with a history dating back over 20,000 years. They lived in small family groups as hunters and gatherers in the harsh environment of the Kalahari Desert. Traditionally, decision-making was by consensus and the society was egalitarian. During the last two centuries, pressure on land from farmers, other ethnic groups, or mining companies all but cut off the San from their traditional lands. Although the majority remained on their ancestral land, they lost all rights to land and other natural resources as new occupants were more successful in obtaining legally recognised ownership, a concept unknown in the San culture (BVLF 2001).

Background: legal-political, socio-economic, educational and linguistic situation

    Because of the enforced changes in their way of living, the San people face many problems. The various San clans used to have enough land to sustain their family bands, while being able to respect territorial borders and avoid conflict with neighbours. Resettlement of families into larger and mostly unrelated groups who now have to share a far-smaller area has brought new challenges. Because of a lack of unity in the settlements, the San, who are now living together in larger groups and with other ethnic groups, do not see themselves as a community. This has hindered most of the development efforts in the settlements, and has made it almost impossible for the school authorities to obtain unanimous decisions from parents, or for the parents to form pressure groups unified against injustices or bad practices.

    This hunter-gatherer people no longer have access to their old territories or the skills to earn a livelihood. They face this situation with a sense of hopelessness and despair; unemployment is high and alcoholism is a serious problem. Consequences can be family structures that no longer support the child, and which can actually become a threat to his or her emotional development.

If the school does not provide sympathetic avenues of communication and assistance, the child may perceive dropping out of school – to go in search of emotional support from the wider community or his or her peers – as the only means of survival.

Government programmes have concentrated on food handouts, rendering this group dependent on relief assistance, while NGOs have given priority to the recognition of the groups' cultural identity (BVLF 2001). Drought Relief projects have taken priority over many other development efforts as a short-term solution to providing food – without creating permanent job opportunities. The people by now are used to interventions of one kind or another that have short-term outcomes.

In the formal education system, the San children meet a different culture and have to cope with conflicting expectations and norms, as well as unfamiliar languages.

It is accepted that the San are the most educationally marginalized group throughout the region, as well as being the most sociologically and economically marginalized. San children are further marginalized in the formal education system in multiple ways, from a lack of mother-tongue instruction in the early years to cultural insensitivity and stigmatization on the part of their peers and often teachers. For various reasons, a high number of San drop out of the formal school system in the respective countries long before completing their secondary or even primary schooling (Yvonne Pickering, personal communication).

The origins of the Bokamoso Pre-school Programme lie in a church-sponsored playgroup started in 1983 at a farm in D'Kar. In 1986, government Drought Relief projects built pre-schools in settlements to which San people had been moved, and the D'Kar staff were asked to manage these settlement schools and monitor the training of teachers.

The general objective of Bokamoso is:

- To enable children from minority groups to have access to quality early childhood care and education so as to adjust to the formal school environment without losing their unique cultural identity.

Bokamoso also aims to reduce the high drop-out rate in primary schools and to foster in parents a positive attitude towards education. It also strives to build the self-esteem of the people by training teachers who originate from the local communities and by involving parents in early childhood care programmes for their children (BVLF 2001).

The Bokamoso Programme incorporates four main hypotheses:

1. that San children who have gone through pre-school would be less likely to drop out of formal schools
2. that parents would participate more positively in the formal education process if their children were somehow 'lured' into learning through play
3. that the introduction of Setswana and English in an informal way would break through children's resistance to other languages and give them a head-start in primary school
4. that the San culture – including languages, musical heritage and oral traditions – has so much to offer to the modern world that the identity and traditional knowledge of the San should be nurtured and promoted in order to enrich modern education systems.

From the start, parents and communities are involved in the early childhood education: the Village Development Committees (VDCs) own the pre-schools. They choose the teachers that Bokamoso trains. The VDCs in Gantsi district get a grant from the Gantsi District Council and use that according to their own decisions for salaries, material and other running costs in the centres. The parents are involved in the daily teaching and asked to assist in putting up playground structures as well as making traditional toys for the children. Bokamoso assists parents and VDCs with these responsibilities, working alongside the Social and Community Development Programme of the Gantsi District Council.

Methods used

The training programme is a two-year in-service course for village teachers who originate from the local communities and have been selected by their communities. Workshops of two weeks each are held three times a year, and field workers regularly visit the schools.

Training is followed up by visits to trainees in the field, to monitor teachers' performance and to assist with practical activities, for example, preparation of the daily programme and use of the Bokamoso Theme Books as references. The pre-school in D'Kar is under direct supervision of Bokamoso, and advice and management support is also given to thirteen pre-schools in the district, run by the Village Development Committees of the local District Council, as well as to two playgroups in Gantsi Township, three playgroups on farms run by parents and a pre-school in Gantsi township, making a total of nineteen early childhood education programmes in the district. Bokamoso also trains teachers of San communities in other districts and monitors their progress.

The Bokamoso Programme also strives to build self-esteem by involving parents in early childhood care and education and sensitizing them to the importance of formal education.

Although not many of the San traditional child-rearing practices are still in operation, belief in them is still very prevalent. The trainers of Bokamoso include traditional stories and games in the teacher training, and the present curriculum has been built from workshops with parents and teachers to document traditional child-

rearing practices that are relevant in modern education.

Parents and grandparents are invited to share their
traditional knowledge of hunting and veld food and to
teach traditional dances and tell stories. Mother-tongue
education is a prerogative and interactive, child-cen-
tred teaching is promoted, based on the free and
non-restrictive childrearing methods the San were
known for.

The pre-schools correspond with the San's
educational traditions of free group activity and exper-
imentation. The fact that the mother tongue is spoken
in each pre-school alongside Setswana, and that the
teachers are mostly chosen from their own community,
adds emotional security.

Naro – being the main San language in the Gantsi district
and the only one with an orthography and a literacy
programme – is the language used in most early-childhood centres. In other pre-schools in the Gantsi district,
the mother tongue is one of the other San languages
(Dcui, Dxana, Qgōo or Tcgaox'ae) or Sekgalagadi.

Language(s) of instruction

The Naro-language team assist the teachers at the
beginning of each year with the spelling of the San
names. Non-San government officials and teachers have
great difficulty with spelling the San names correctly.
This results in many different spellings for the same
name or the same spelling for many different names. To
counteract this confusion, the Naro team assists all the
early-childhood centres and primary schools – and even
health facilities – at the beginning of the year with registering the new names of the children. In the
pre-schools the children then receive a name badge to
teach them the correct spelling of their name.

In primary schools, on the other hand, because
of the culture and language gap, the teachers often find
it difficult to form a relationship with the child, which
has a negative effect on the learning process. San children

mostly do not understand Setswana, and the teachers have no knowledge of the San languages.

Thus teachers of Standards 1 and 2 are at a loss as to how to communicate the required learning material to these children in time for them to pass up to the next level. People working with the San do not regard it as important to gain enough knowledge about the people and their culture and language. This gives the children the perception that their own culture is inferior, and it affects their self-esteem.

Curriculum/Themes The Bokamoso trainers and teachers, in co-operation with the parents and communities, have developed theme books that cover the main educational areas. The themes covered are: 'veld' (food), 'animals', 'my home', 'my body', 'ways of transport' and 'the seasons', as well as a religious education theme book. These books are used by the teachers during preparations of the daily programme. They include traditional knowledge, songs, games, plays and stories concerning the theme.

Teachers/Training The Bokamoso Team includes a Co-ordinator and Assistant Co-ordinator (Botswana) and a San trainer, as well as three San Community Motivators who train teachers during workshops as well as provide hands-on support to teachers, and who work with parents in their respective communities.

Bokamoso is the only Early Childhood Educators' Training Programme in the region with San trainers. A remarkable achievement is that these trainers started off as San pre-school teachers themselves, then gradually excelled to be appointed as trainers – a motivating factor for teachers, as it helps with the ownership of the programme. These San trainers also act as in-house consultants on San culture and traditional education methods.

Trainees to become village teachers have been selected by their communities, who are represented by the Parent-Teacher Associations. The pre-schools are co-ordinated by Village Development Committees who in turn fall under the Social and Community Development Office of the local District Councils.

Networking with the Government and other NGOs in the region is extremely important for the sake of promoting better understanding of the work of Boka-moso (and of KFO) in the light of sensitivity about ethnic-specific programmes. For this reason, the Boka-moso co-ordinator regularly attended District Council meetings in the past year, worked with the District Department of Social and Community Development in assisting communities to run and manage their own pre-schools, and also worked with the District Educa-tion Office. In addition, she attended the Breakthrough Infant Teachers Workshop and conducted a Primary-School Teachers' Workshop in order to explain the aims of Bokamoso and the problems of the San children in their schools (WIMSA, p. 7).

Materials and activities

The Training Co-ordinator and one of the Community Motivators attended a week-long Early-Childhood Trainers' Network Conference for Southern Africa, in Windhoek, organized by Maud's College in Norway (WIMSA, p. 7).

The trainers have over the years developed a cur-riculum and a trainers' manual for the two-year training. In each workshop, trainees are introduced to the Boka-moso Theme books, and material making is an important part of the training. The programme stimu-lates trainees to use local and waste materials in toy-making. Dolls have been made out of clothes and grass; necklaces of seeds; and puzzles, games and chairs using cardboard boxes.

The Programme assists the pre-schools with the administration of the grants they receive from the Gov-ernment, as well as helping to raise funds for other needs of the schools.

Bokamoso also advises non-San communities on

starting up pre-schools, trains teachers from other districts, and holds activities to create community awareness and parent interaction in the settlements.

Further activities include:

Playgroups on Farms
Bokamoso is working with the Farm Workers' Project of the local District Council and the Workers' Committees on farms, to monitor the welfare and school attendance of children of the workers. Seven farms now receive training for parents, and the Community Motivators of Bokamoso do follow-up field visits together with the Farm Workers' Project Advisor.

Parent support and training
The Bokamoso Programme also strives to build self-esteem, involving parents in early childhood care and education and sensitizing them to the importance of formal education. Community Leaders and Parents' Workshops are held in all settlements, villages and farms with an early-childhood education programme. Topics included HIV/AIDS, craft-making, literacy classes, material development, the importance of education, and how children learn and develop, as well as stressing the need for parent involvement in their children's schooling (WIMSA, p. 9).

Primary-school teachers' sensitization workshops
Most primary-school teachers in schools with a San student population belong to another, more powerful ethnic group in Botswana and are ignorant of, and biased against, San culture and language. Bokamoso tries to introduce the different aspects of San culture to them to enable them to have a better communication with their students. In co-operation with the Naro-language team, Naro-language courses with tapes and text books are offered to interested teachers.

Tertiary and Vocational Skills Training
Each of the KFO organizations has several inservice training programmes for capacity building, aimed at helping San youths bridge the gap to tertiary education.

Letloa, for example, is assisting the KFO to develop a community development facilitator (CDF) training course to enable youths to fulfil positions in their own Community Based Organization (CBO) and/or become resource people for their communities. Ten candidates were appointed as trainees in several of the KFO members, and the first workshop was held in May 2002. A two-year in-service course, broken into several modules, will start full-scale in 2003, and entry into upgrading programmes for their secondary-school qualifications will form part of this course. (The CDF course is not to be confused with other in-service training courses for San staff in the KFO, which are designed to enhance the San's capacity in their own job situation.)

The CDFs are community members affiliated to San CBOs who are served by the KFO members in different communities in Gantsi and Ngamiland districts. The CDFs will be trained to become staff or community leaders in their respective communities.

Examples from other such capacity-building courses for KFO staff include the in-service training of four San women, which enabled them to graduate from being pre-school teachers to becoming trainers and community motivators for Bokamoso. Bokamoso was also offered a full scholarship by the Mindolo Ecumenical Foundation in Zambia for a three-month Certificate Course in Specialized Care and Management of Orphans and Vulnerable Children. And one of the trainers participated in the PR course offered by WIMSA and TUCSIN in Namibia (WIMSA, p. 12).

BOKAMOSO EARLY CHILDCARE AND DEVELOPMENT (ECD) TEACHER TRAINING

Over 100 local people have been trained as early-childhood educators

Outcomes

The present ECD Training Programme is under threat, as the new policy of the Ministry of Education requests training for pre-school teachers to diploma level. Most of the trainees chosen by their communities to become pre-school teachers did not finish their senior secondary school and thus do not qualify for a diploma course. However, Bokamoso is committed to providing training of community members as long as there are community-run centres (WIMSA, p. 7).

Of seven teachers who enrolled in the last two years only two completed, due to the problems of getting these community schools funded and the lack of a clear policy for support from the Government.

In the San communities a greater involvement of parents in the education of their children and a clear feeling of ownership of the pre-schools is a clear result of Bokamoso's training.

The Social and Community Development Department of the Gantsi District Council, however, tends to see the involvement of Bokamoso with pre-schools as interfering with their work and responsibilities. The S&CD Department thus sometimes takes trainees out of the Bokamoso training and sends them to a government-supported institute.

Findings of the tracer study

A study carried out in 1994/5 on children who had been in pre-schools and who were traced in Standards 1 to 4, in seven primary schools, found a total of 172 such children, the majority in Standard 1 (63) and Standard 2 (70).

The children who had attended pre-schools were mostly still in school, many parents were supportive of formal education, and some head teachers were trying to adapt the school to the realities of the community.

One of the schools in the study has boarding facilities, and large numbers of children were sent there in 1995 at a very young age. Many of them returned home after the first few weeks or even days, or did not return to school after the first term. At another school, a very sympathetic headmistress seemed to have accepted the lifestyle of the parents, and had tried to adapt the school to the realities of the community.

Although quite a few children still dropped out in the course of a year, the registers showed most of these children returning to school the next year, or even two years later.

Lack of food was given by both teachers and parents as a major reason for children dropping out of school. The fact that in the early 1990s the Bokamoso Programme organized meals at each school was considered by many as one of the reasons children stayed in the pre-schools.

For children staying with their parents, the traditional lack of a daily routine for meals, bedtime and other activities creates problems when they have to attend school. San, as a rule, never had organized meal times, but would often walk and eat while gathering food, or eat in the veld where they found food. This pattern is still quite prevalent as far as gathering is concerned. Instead of coming home (from school) to find that they have missed out on the day's harvest, children prefer to follow their mother to the veld.

An analysis of enrolments, repetition rates and drop-outs in seven schools in the Gantsi District between 1997 and 2000 found that the highest numbers of children dropped out of school from Standard 1.

Numbers of drop-outs then tend to decrease as children move up through the different classes. There was a high repetition rate in Standard 4, explained by the fact that this level is the first at which children are held back on the basis of their academic performance. Those who repeat in Standards 1 to 3 are generally children who had dropped out the previous year and have to start the year again.

The enrolment and drop-out rates, in absolute numbers and in percentages, varied quite widely from school to school and from year to year. From this it was surmised that factors such as an individual teacher or the atmosphere in a school influence the children. The drop-out figures for the only school in the study with a boarding hostel had improved since figures were collected in 1993–5.

One possible explanation for this is that since most of the other primary schools now go up to at least Standard 4, children are able to stay with their families for their first school years before boarding, therefore separation from their parents takes place later and is less traumatic.

It was also found that slightly more girls were enrolled in primary school than boys and that the girls tended to stay in school more than the boys. The drop-out rate for boys was higher than for girls in all the schools except one, where the rates were nearly identical and relatively high. Overall, the girls had a drop-out rate of 8.5 per cent, whereas the boys had a drop-out rate of 12.3 per cent.

Lessons learnt: strengths and weaknesses

Although the pre-schools are perceived as successful, this may even aggravate negative feelings towards the primary school. The pre-school has now become the 'model' against which the primary school is judged. If parents learn from these pre-schools that there are other ways of practising 'modern' education – without spanking the children, for example – they might more readily accept the reasons children give for dropping out of primary school. Their consent to established primary schools and withdrawal of participation from the 'modern' pre-schools weaken the chances of change in the primary schools. This would benefit neither the institutions nor the children.

However, in most cases, San parents feel that once they have 'given' their children to the school, they have lost control over them. When the children go to school, they enter a different world, and the parents then sometimes even feel inferior to their own children. Their lack of understanding creates mistrust that often turns into excessively aggressive behaviour towards the teachers, when parents suspect them of mistreatment or favouritism. Many still believe that they are doing the government a favour by allowing their children to go to school in the first place.

The WIMSA report *Torn Apart: San Children as Change Agents in a Process of Acculturation* (1999) reflects broadly on San children in education all over the southern African region. The overriding impression of the researchers was the similarity of the situation everywhere, regardless of the efforts to improve the situation and counter the appalling school drop-out rate. The title of the report, *Torn Apart*, was chosen because it became apparent that the San children are the victims of two opposing forces involved in their education process. Teachers, as well as extension and health workers, on the one side, and parents and communities on the other, all expect the children to bring about socio-economic change for the San people and to provide a basis for political power. Each side endeavours to reach their goal through the children.

The five main themes/issues that were emphasised by the San people were: power and dependency, poverty, abuse and discrimination, language, and cultural differences.

The tracer study reached six main conclusions:

1.   The language gap in the primary schools is a main reason that San children leave school early.

2. Corporal punishment in schools is counterproductive to the progress of the children and was shown by the survey as the single most direct reason for children leaving school.

3. It might be that the objective of preparing pre-school children for primary school has resulted in highlighting, by comparison, the problems in primary schools, thus creating animosity and tension.

4. There is a serious lack of cultural understanding between San parents/communities and teachers.

5. Education touches the heart of a culture, and the education system has to adapt to the specific situation at each place, address the realities of the children's lives, and assist children in distress.

6. Feeding schemes in primary schools, despite the danger of increasing dependency, could remove a stumbling block towards Education for All in the short term, while the dividends of a better education would re-establish the balance in the long term.

Duration

The Bokamoso teacher-training programme began in 1988 and had been affiliated to the larger Kuru Training Centre, which was started in 1991, but recently became independent.

Funding/Budget

Bernard van Leer Foundation, the Netherlands; Christian Reformed Churches in the Netherlands; and some other small donors.

Responsible organization(s)

Kuru Family of Organizations (KFO)
Letloa Support Organization
WIMSA (Working Group of Indigenous Minorities in Southern Africa)

Contact

For Bokamoso:
Gaolatlhe Thupe
Co-ordinator, Bokamoso Programme
P.O. Box 925

Gantsi
Botswana
Tel +267 6596574
E-mail: gantsibokamoso@botsnet.bw

For Letloa:
Willemien le Roux
Education and Cultural Advisor for Kuru Family of
Organizations c/o Letloa
P.O. Box 472
Shakawe
Botswana
Tel/fax: +267 6875084/5
E-mail: wleroux@botsnet.bw

*Special thanks go to Willemien le Roux and the Bokamoso
Team who revised and amended the draft of this case study.
Additional information has been included where indicated
from the following sources:*

- WIMSA (Working Group of Indigenous Minori-
  ties in Southern Africa), on behalf of its partners
  in Botswana, Namibia and South Africa: 'Progress
  Report on a Regional San Education and Culture
  Programme (RSCEP), under auspices of WIMSA,
  November 1998 – December 2002'
- Bernard Van Leer Foundation: PROJECT
  DESCRIPTIONS 2001-BVLF. Retrieved from
  http://www.bernardvanleer.org
- Informal information by Yvonne Pickering,
  WIMSA, Namibia
- The webpage of the Kuru Family of Organiza-
  tions: http://www.san.org.za

NOTES:

1. The main part of the information presented in this case study is based on excerpts of
   a summary report (The challenges of change: a tracer study of San pre-school children

in Botswana) of a study carried out from 1993 to 1995 that traced San children of primary-school age who had participated in the Bokamoso Pre-school Programme, including an update to 2001 containing additional background information and new findings by Willemien le Roux: Willemien le Roux (2002), Early Childhood Development: Practice and Reflections No. 15, The Hague, Bernard van Leer Foundation. Retrieved from http://www.bernardvanleer.org

BRAZIL:
THE AUTHORSHIP EXPERIENCE AMONG INDIGENOUS PEOPLES OF THE BRAZILIAN WESTERN AMAZON

Nietta Lindenberg Monte

Intercultural Bilingual Programme for the Training of Indigenous Teachers and Agroforest Agents through formal and informal training

Type of programme and educational level

Fourteen municipalities, twenty-eight indigenous territories in three states of Western Amazon (Acre, Amazônia and Rondônia), Brazil; government supported NGO programme

Geographical and administrative level

One hundred and seventeen indigenous teachers of twelve indigenous nations belonging to three linguistic families:

Indigenous target groups

- Eight from the Panoan family: Kaxinawa, Katukina, Yawanawa, Jaminawa, Shanenawa, Shawadawa, Poyanawa, Kaxarari
- Three from the Aruak family: Manchineri, Ashaninka, Apurina
- One from the Arawa: Kulina

Around 5,000 students have been participating in the programme since 1983 through the forest schools; some of these proceeded on to the teacher training and others became the sixty-eight agroforest agents. The total indigenous population benefiting from this programme comprises about 10,000 persons.

Description of Programme

Summary

The programme 'An Authorship Experience' of the Pro-Indigenous Commission of Acre (CPI/AC) – one of the oldest non-governmental organizations in Brazil – aims at supporting the indigenous societies in the Amazon region in their search for cultural, social, economic and environmental sustainability through the training of personnel as actors in the areas of education, health and environment.

The educational programme started in 1983, linked to wider political issues such as the demarcation of indigenous territories and their sustainable development, and the organization of indigenous co-operatives and associations. The main activity consists of in-service training courses for bilingual indigenous teachers of different nations of the Western Amazon, in order to enable teachers to formulate and practice a new kind of education for their students, and to promote the revitalization of their forest schools. One of the main elements of this in-service training is the creation and production of textbooks and other educational material by the indigenous teacher-students, their students and communities. A new curriculum and around eighty textbooks have been created and produced by the indigenous teachers in partnership with their tutors from the Pro-Indigenous Commission of Acre and advisers of several universities of the country.

In recent years, students of the indigenous forest schools participating in the programme have been trained to become agroforest agents, so that they progressively become more aware of local environmental problems, and think and act toward the solution of these problems within both local and global perspectives.

Background: legal-political, socio-economic, educational and linguistic situation

The Brazilian Constitution, promulgated in 1988, recognizes that indigenous peoples have specific rights, differentiated from those of the non-indigenous population; accordingly, specific legislation and educational policies have been elaborated and implemented since the end of the 1990s. These developments were supported and boosted by the mobilization and increasing political articulation and organization of indigenous peoples, with the support of their allies in civil society, leading to the creation of new indigenous associations and organizations. In accordance with the principles established in the Constitution, a specific legislation was ratified in 1996. As regards indigenous educational rights, the Lei de Diretrizes e Bases (LDB – Basis and Guidelines Act) for Brazilian Education affirms the right of indigenous peoples to intercultural bilingual education. Article 87 of the LDB deals with the training and empowerment of all teachers in practice/service – be they indigenous or not – and states that formal and complete training of all teachers is an obligation of the Federal State (Union), of the states and municipalities.

This new national legislation provides the basis for the autonomy of the indigenous schools regarding the creation of their curricula and the study in their own languages and in Portuguese, as well as the right to decide on their own process of learning.

SOCIOLINGUISTIC SITUATION

Two of the indigenous nations participating in the programme are monolingual in Portuguese, with very few individuals (the elders) who can speak their indigenous language, and then often only well enough for educational purposes but not for daily social functions: the Shawadawa and Poyanawa. Three nations are bilingual, with dominance in Portuguese: the Shanenawa, Yawanawa and Apurina. And seven Indigenous Nations are bilingual, with dominance in indigenous languages: the

Kaxinawa, Katukina, Manchineri, Ashaninka, Jaminawa, Kaxarari and Kulina.

More than half of the indigenous population of Acre (approx. 5,876 people) continue to actively practice their language and culture in their daily life. On the other hand, we observe a tendency of change in the younger generations, especially in territories near the villages of the municipalities, where the young adults and children do not speak their indigenous language, but can understand it, and where only the elders can speak the language in special situations related to their traditional culture or for political issues (this applies to around 2,113 people).

Objectives and focus

The overall objective of the programme is to build and strengthen critical and reflexive capacities so that the teachers and agroforest agents, and their communities as a whole, can identify the socio-environmental problems of their territories within a national and international context, and think and act collectively to find solutions, by means of environmental and intercultural bilingual education, both in formal and informal situations.

The focus of the programme is on:

- The learning of indigenous oral and written languages through their active use in the educational process, via both creative and academic tasks that are shared among the indigenous students of different nations and mother tongues
- The production of textbooks, sculptures, paintings, videos, music presentations, etc., as part of the school curriculum; some of this material is also being used at non-indigenous schools, approved by the Ministry of Education as part of the material for teaching the Intercultural Issue to all Brazilian citizens
- The registering and systematizing of ethnic traditional knowledge by teachers, their students, and agroforest agents through research in several sub-

jects such as cosmology or science as a basis for the new indigenous curriculum and textbooks

• The provision of access to occidental or universal contemporary knowledge, values and technologies – such as health practices, agricultural tools, or the recording of music and history on tape or video – which are considered important to students' daily lives and their relation with other languages, cultures and societies.

All the indigenous students to be trained as teachers and agroforest agents are selected and nominated by their communities. During the process of their professional training they also become members of the public staff, receiving remuneration for their work at the schools and communities from the State Secretariat for Education and Culture. In this way, they are socially controlled by the communities and parents, who can express their agreement or disagreement with the work at school to the public system of education by means of collective strategies such as written statements and letters, or orally in meetings, visits to the authorities, and so on.

Participation

The communities (elders, crafters, singers, traditional doctors and so on) play an important part in decision-making regarding the curriculum and the elaboration of textbooks, as they participate in the research of traditional ethnic subjects representing the origin of the knowledge systematized in books, videos, and other materials at the schools.

The work is developed jointly by two local indigenous organizations: the Organization of Indigenous Teachers of Acre (OPIAC), which is structured legally and which emerged as a result of the efforts of mobilization of teachers participating in the education project promoted by CPI/AC, and the Association of the Movement of the Agroforest-Agents (AMAIAC), created recently. As two politically representative entities, OPIAC and AMAIAC aim at promoting and establishing an indigenous education, which is specific and differentiated, as national, regional and local public policy, and work for the protection of the land and economic, environmental and cultural sustainability in accordance with the needs of each ethnic group. Additionally, in their joint effort CPI/AC, OPIAC and AMAIAC are working with various indigenous associations of an ethnic-regional character such as APIWTXA (Associação Ashaninka do rio Amônia), ASKAPA (Associação dos Kaxinawá da Praia do Carapanã), ASKARJ (Associação dos Seringueiros Kaxinawá do Rio Jordão), and ASAYRG (Associação Yawanawá do Rio Gregório).

Methods used

The indigenous educational actors utilize the 'Centre for the Training of Forest People' (a rural area owned by CPI/AC) as a training space for teachers and agroforest agents. This Centre is a demonstration area and pedagogical model, and theoretical and practical elements of environmental management of the indigenous territories that are already demarcated or in the process of demarcation are included in the work of the educational actors.

The concept and methods of the programme focus on the 'authorship of indigenous people', as individuals and collectively, and on the different aspects of educational, linguistic, environmental and cultural decisions, as important elements of the self-determination of indigenous nations. Indigenous languages and Portuguese, and other non-verbal traditional means of communication and expression – such as graphic arts, sculpture, music and performance – are transversally used in the intercultural education process to revitalize, transmit and increase the value of the teacher/students' own culture in the necessary dialogue with other cultures and languages. The training courses offered to teacher/students and agroforest agents allow for reflection and dialogue among the participants of diverse indigenous cultures and their non-indigenous tutors and advisers. They are based on the indigenous knowledge about different areas of interest, such as health, environment, subsistence practices, resource management and oral traditions. This knowledge is interpreted through new forms of articulation and expression (verbal, graphical, audio-visual) and through indigenous languages as well as Portuguese. This creates a momentum for teachers and agents, who act as multiplicators, to access the knowledge of other peoples as a means of widening their capacity to reflect about their realities and to develop collective strategies for the solution of problems which currently affect their communities.

'Attendant' (intensive training courses) and 'non-attendant' (training in the villages, where teachers and agroforest agents continue to live, study and work) training generates *four modalities* of educational situations that are used for the training of the indigenous teachers and agroforest agents:

- Intensive annual courses: Courses of around 300 hours at the 'Centre for the Training of Forest People', where the indigenous teacher and agroforest students of different nations and mother tongues come together for two months of the year during their training (January and February for the teachers, and July to August for the agroforest agents) to meet and exchange their knowledge and practices in schools and in environmental actions, with the mediation of non-Indian advisers and tutors of different areas – language, mathematics, geography, history, anthropology, biology, etc.
- Rotating workshops: Workshops offered in the indigenous lands or villages for about a month each year by the advisers and tutors of the programme, allowing for the assessment and evaluation of the work and of the problems experienced by each indigenous teacher and agroforest agent with their students and communities in the local context.
- Autonomous reflexive work by the teachers and agroforest agents which is promoted throughout the year to enable them to plan and evaluate their

action at school and in the communities. This includes different research activities on locally specific subjects such as agricultural, health or religious practices, and intercultural universal themes/subjects such as human rights, mathematics or geography, which together form the basis for producing textbooks, videos and other educational material.

One of the main elements of this reflexive work is the writing down of the daily memories of their work in the communities during the year in special notebooks, including information on socio-cultural practices such as fishing, hunting, and the use and management of natural resources or ceremonies, as well as information on personal and community-related experiences with regard to their work, student behaviour, research results or problems encountered. The teachers and agroforest agents then take these notebooks or diaries back to the intensive courses in the city, so as to exchange their notes and reflections with the other teacher-students and agroforest-agent-students as part of their training, in this way linking theory and practice, thought and action, cultural and intercultural knowledge.

- *Exchanges and visits* between indigenous teachers and agroforest agents are also supported as part of their training, enabling them to reflect about different realities and contexts, similarities and differences, so that they can collectively shape the common issues of intercultural education and environmental action.

Languages of instruction

All tutors and advisers of the training courses are committed to encouraging the use of indigenous languages as a form of expression for teachers and students, and as a means of developing any theme or area of knowledge. Most of the teacher-students also agree on the valuable role played by language in history, memory and identity. Most of them give significant consideration to their language when designing their school curriculum and when structuring their plan of course as a reflexive exercise in the training situations. However, in the day-to-day practice of the school curriculum, the place assigned to, and the use of, indigenous languages and Portuguese are also determined by other factors, such as the attitudes and preferences of the community concerning language, the origin and availability of the materials used (both in Portuguese and indigenous languages), and the visits of tutors of CPI/AC or the Department of Education.

As mentioned above, there exists a great sociolinguistic diversity in Acre: seven nations participating in the programme are BDIL, three are BDPL and two MPL. Therefore, the level and extension of the use of indigenous languages and Portuguese in the school curriculum varies from one community to another according to each community's historical conditions and perspectives, and attitudes and preferences regarding language and identity. Thus, there is more than one model for the use of language in the curriculum, as the diversity and the heterogeneity of the sociolinguistic situations are part of the nature of the school's social realities and their representation in the curriculum.

- In the case of the ten indigenous nations that are bilingual, the indigenous languages are normally used together with Portuguese in a flexible way at various levels of their studies to construct and transmit curriculum subjects such as history, geography, language and literature.
- The two nations that are monolingual in Portuguese are learning and studying their indigenous languages in the specific situations where they are still used, such as religion and ritual music, and in a few intercommunication contexts, such as naming things in hunting, fishing or eating.
- Some of the indigenous nations, especially those

bilingual indigenous nations with dominance in their indigenous language, are undertaking efforts to record different aspects of their identities, including oral histories, music, religion and art. This is done through research with the few remaining speakers, the production of alphabets and graphic systems, as well as the creation of important documents for school curriculum, such as primers, songbooks or storybooks.

Curriculum/Themes

The curriculum is understood as a historical process of collective construction involving indigenous leaders, teachers, agroforest agents, their advisers and tutors, and the institutions with which they work. It has to respond to the daily problems they identify now and will identify in the future, such as the social and environmental pressures on their natural, linguistic and cultural resources. The curriculum emphasizes and reflects their research and reflections on the biological, social and linguistic diversity of their local world as related to global problems as a whole. In this respect, their knowledge concerning the management of the forest and of other natural resources is revitalized and revalued, especially through the involvement of the elders.

As a result of this process of work, the curriculum for the training courses has three main transversal themes: language, culture, and land/environment.

Curriculum subjects and contents include:

- Different areas of local knowledge, such as the cartography of indigenous reserves, the research of still-existing and protected animals and plants, or even the study of the grammar and use of indigenous languages
- Subjects related to the particular history or cosmology of each group, their specific language patterns or material culture
- General subjects of common concern to all indigenous groups in Brazil, such as the issue of

colonization, the loss of indigenous lands, and indigenous peoples' struggle for their rights, and

• More universal themes such health, environment or human rights.

Curricula contents and subjects are represented in written material in indigenous languages and in Portuguese, and in several patterns and styles of documentation, such as short stories with drawings, performances, sculptures or videos. They stimulate the recording and promulgation of mythical narratives, music and other traditional aspects, including knowledge about flora and fauna, concepts of space and time, and contemporary and difficult themes such as AIDS, the threat to water resources, slavery, etc. The use of such contemporary themes has led to the generation of a new kind of textbook involving transversal themes defined in the Curricular Reference for Indigenous Schools (cultural diversity, rights, education and health, biodiversity etc.) and to the study areas of curricular programmes in indigenous schools (languages, mathematics, geography etc.).

We can observe a great level of autonomy on the part of the schools in the decision-making regarding the designing of curricula and the use of time and space. For example, vacation times are adjusted according to families' and communities' agricultural activities such as planting and harvesting, so that students can participate in these activities and thereby learn from family and friends about their culture, while at the same time having a break from the classroom.

Teachers

The mainly non-indigenous tutors and advisers of the programme are mostly teachers from various Brazilian universities who come once or twice a year to participate in the intensive training courses in the city of Rio Branco. They are also in charge of editing and organizing the textbooks based on the texts and drawings produced by the teachers in the course of their in-service training.

The indigenous teacher and agroforest students are young adult and adult men and women who were chosen by their communities to be trained as teachers and agroforest agents and who started their educational career teaching the literacy courses provided (since 1983) by the Pro-Indigenous Commission Education Program. However, owing to the role of women in their traditional culture, only 10 per cent of the teacher-students are women, and all of the agroforest students are male. These students study for two months of the year in the state capital and receive visits from other teachers and from their advisers during the year in their villages, where they give classes to the first grades of primary level, as outlined in the section on 'methods used'.

Up to now, forty-seven of these teacher-students have received their official certificate as bilingual and intercultural teachers corresponding to the medium degree, having participated in around 6,000 hours of training courses and the other modalities of learning situations. They are now able to enter the two universities in Brazil that have recently started to prepare indigenous teachers for bilingual and intercultural education. Three of the indigenous teachers of Acre are already enrolled in superior training in one of these universities in another state of Brazil and will be able to teach the second part of the primary level and the secondary level to their students.

Materials and activities Around eighty indigenous textbooks were developed as educational materials during these training activities by the indigenous teachers and their students and other members of their communities, with the co-operation of their advisers. The books, written in Portuguese and indigenous languages, cover various areas of interest in culturally and interculturally relevant subjects and have become a fundamental part of the pedagogical methods and the curricula of indigenous-teacher-training programmes.

This material has fulfilled the very important purpose of creating and expanding the concept of a new kind of written literature transmitted in indigenous languages and Portuguese, as well as branching into new forms of cultural media, such as video, CD-ROM etc. This material has in turn been used to carry out research on both new and ancient knowledge, its documentation and diffusion.

Collective means of production

During the stages of training referred to as 'attendant' (intensive training courses) and 'non-attendant' (completed in the villages, where participants continue to live, study and work), the indigenous teachers themselves (and now also the indigenous students being trained in other professional areas, such as health and forestry) generate the educational material. Sometimes this material is the result of studies developed by indigenous teachers of different ethnic groups and mother tongues, which nevertheless focuses on one specific area of knowledge. In these cases, the texts are usually in Portuguese, since, owing to the different linguistic background of the participants, it is the main language of communication in these courses. In other cases, members of the same ethnic group and mother tongue develop texts in their own language.

These texts may include descriptions of special activities experienced during the courses or taking place in the participants' daily lives with their clan throughout the year (such as the diaries mentioned above).

Content vs. didactic potential of the material

The textbooks must also be able to reflect, in their conception and development, the methodological and curricular guidance of the training courses, and so create a bridge between the study content in the training courses and the teaching procedure in indigenous schools. They can thus be of great use to the author-teachers as references for class content and pedagogical procedures that are employed in schools, and as such are fundamental tools in the teaching and learning process. In their schools, the teachers will be working with teaching methods, and their implementation, that they themselves helped develop and apply during the conception of the texts.

Research and production of material

Research activities are fundamental for the production of materials. The advisers and tutors of the training programmes have encouraged research and have implemented the means for the development of these literary works by discussing methodology and organizing manuscripts in co-operation with the teachers. Most of the time the indigenous teachers do not master all aspects of their culture. Through research involving other members of the community, they have the opportunity to organize information about their specific cultures, and to widen their own knowledge in the process.

Research allows teachers to deepen and develop the themes to be addressed in the final texts, while leading them to suggest and discuss different versions; it promotes the appreciation of classification systems, and it helps identify cultural taboos, which must be respected when the texts are put down on paper and released to the public. It is up to the individual communities, therefore, to decide what part of their own culture should be represented and published and which languages should be used.

Another reason for doing research during teacher training is to direct participants towards knowledge that is not unique to certain communities, nor part of their social past, but which constitutes a common good. This includes scientific, cultural and historical research that supports an informed intercultural dialogue and the creation of a critical point of view regarding the social and historical foundations of the modern world.

Co-operation between specialists: a partnership of indigenous and non-indigenous authors

Tutors who are specialists in the various areas concerned in the training courses take part at every level of the production of didactic material. These specialists advise the indigenous authors on data classification, format, and selection of texts for illustration. They include tutors who participate in the teacher-training programmes, as well as professionals from universities, etc., who assist the teacher-students in their educational process during the exchanges and visits mentioned above. Moreover, the development of these texts must be encouraged not only in the confines of the classrooms but also during the 'non-attendant' phases of the course, when a greater number of decisions need to be taken by the indigenous teachers themselves, together with the elder members of their communities.

GENERAL OUTCOMES

In 1985, all the forest schools that had been created by the indigenous communities with the commencement **Outcomes** of the training courses (supported by the programme since 1983) became part of the public education system of the state of Acre. They were registered as indigenous bilingual schools, and their intercultural curriculum and textbooks were recognized and legitimized as indigenous education for the primary level (Grades 1 – 4). In addition, the training courses for indigenous teachers and agroforest agents are recognized, and partially supported, by the Brazilian State. This marked the first time in Brazilian indigenous history that a civil society organization, such as CPI/AC, acting independently of the official indigenous agency FUNAI (the National Indigenous Foundation), and the various religious missions, was recognized by the Department of Education as an organization providing services, not only for teaching literacy, but for medium-level indigenous-teacher training.

Some of the indigenous demands and procedures regarding educational practices, curricula content, autonomy of schools, and indigenous training courses – as well as schools and land rights – have resulted in new federal, state and municipal laws, and the encouragement of new policies towards indigenous peoples. These advances have been the fruit of growing co-operation between the indigenous communities, government organs, and society as a whole.

An important differential concept of the Intercultural Bilingual Education in Brazil, resulting from the Acrean programme, is that of 'authorship', which expresses the political idea of the 'self-determination' of the indigenous peoples in educational, linguistic and cultural fields. This concept has been important in the Brazilian education reform carried out over the last few years, in that it has sustained an overhaul of curricula in indigenous schools, and because it not only constitutes an important vehicle for the learning of written languages by societies that traditionally express themselves solely in an oral manner, but also enables indigenous teachers-in-training to have access to new knowledge, and to resources for study and research, which can consequently be passed on to their students. In this manner, these indigenous teachers and students are able to free themselves from the shackles of colonial (and post-colonial) era schooling and of knowledge conveyed in dominant languages not their own, and therefore become beings of their own making, fulfilling an important role as researchers, formulators and interpreters of relevant knowledge composed and fashioned for other cultural contexts as well as their own.

Indigenous training and material

Presently, the state of Acre has some forty-seven indigenous teachers with the title of Indigenous Teacher of medium level – with another 150 teacher-students to be completing their studies and receiving their title in 2005 – thanks to the Authorship Project of the Pro-Indigenous Commission of Acre, CPI/AC. This has led to a pioneering and innovative curriculum proposal in the country, elaborated and systematized by CPI/AC, approved by the responsible state organism, the Federal Education Council of Acre (CEE/AC), and recognized as a reference for wider public policies by the Ministry of Education.

The indigenous teachers, together with their students and parents, are representatives of important improvements in terms of literacy and the range of knowledge provided to a group of around 5,000 students, youths and adults of both sexes, during the last twenty years. This means that about half of the indigenous population of the state of Acre, with the support of other actors, institutions and entities, are today in a position of increased opportunities to participate in the benefits and challenges related to the goods and services offered to them in an inter-ethnic context.

This programme counts on innovative pedagogical and didactic resources, such as a set of ninety-four sources of authorship material by indigenous teachers and students, advisers and consultants, edited and distributed in their entirety, in indigenous languages and Portuguese, covering such diverse areas of study as geography, history, science, mathematics and others.

It is worth noting that some of the textbooks produced by indigenous societies, galvanized by local projects, have been distributed all around the country by means of a special programme established by the Ministry of Education called the 'Teacher's Library'. There have also been ground-breaking cases in which texts written by groups of indigenous teachers from Acre have become required reading material in certain circles: 100,000 young Brazilians in Rio Branco, the county's third-largest city were required to read a book called *Shenipabu Miyui, Ancient Stories*, containing illustrations and a collection of ancient stories, published in a bilingual edition and written by the Kaxinawá teachers. It was part of the examination requirements for their entrance to the public university in their city. A new Kaxinawá book was brought out in 2002, and in the same year it officially represented Brazil at the International Book Fair in Geneva, with the full support of the Ministry of Education. Researched and written entirely in indigenous languages, it contains legends about human and indigenous origins.

Furthermore, the authorship project generated three different lines of training, all of them professionalizing: the training of 130 health agents (between 1986 and 1999), of 68 agroforest agents (from 1996 to the present), and 7 indigenous teachers in video and filmmaking (from 1998 to the present) – the latter being realized in partnership between the NGO Vídeo-nas-Aldeias and CPI/AC. In all those cases, the teaching of reading and writing was mainly carried out in the forest schools by indigenous teachers trained in the project. There, they received special literacy instruction in both their own language and in Portuguese and were instructed to a basic competence in mathematics, social and historical studies, leading to the various new professional careers such as health agents, agroforest agents, administrators of co-operatives and associations, and young teachers who are living in their lands, prouder of their identities, and reproducing and transmitting their language, culture and knowledge about the world.

National Policy

The Brazilian government has become conscious of the importance of this kind of local indigenous policy to construct democratic values and plurality, and to assure that indigenous peoples can live and revitalize their culture and agriculture in their lands and create new economic activities in a sustainable manner. There are new policy lines for programmes in the Ministry of Education, Ministry of Environment, Ministry of Health and Ministry of Culture that provide funds and technical support to projects and programmes for the indigenous associations and the NGOs that work in this kind of educational activity.

On the other hand, it was by means of technical support from professionals from CPI/AC that the Ministry of Education elaborated two of their most important technical documents of recent years oriented towards the educational policy for indigenous peoples, documents which would become the National Curriculum Reference for Indigenous Schools (1998) and the Reference for the Training of Indigenous Teachers (2002), both co-ordinated by the founder and pedagogical co-ordinator of the authorship programme.

Local Indigenous Policies

The teachers trained or in training in the state of Acre today find themselves politically and legally organized in the Organization of Indigenous Teachers of Acre (OPIAC), with whom CPI/AC develops various types of partnerships. As this group of teachers today is directly supported and advised by the Authorship Project of CPI/AC, a large number of teachers have moved on to receive further training from the Secretariat of Education of Acre since 2000, with some 180 teachers currently undergoing initial training as Differentiated Teachers, through which they are receiving specific medium-level training in the federal and municipal system.

Legislation

Various new laws have been created – at the national, regional and district level – as a result of the influence of this programme and of other programmes of a similar nature throughout the country. This new legislation is opening up possibilities for the indigenous schools to construct autonomous models in their pedagogical and curriculum proposals with regard to the organization of time and space, the selection of relevant contents and subjects for their school, the methodologies of learning, the languages of instruction, systems of evaluation, the production and selection of textbooks, and the training of teachers.

The relations with the community

Lessons learnt: strengths and weaknesses

It is important, and yet difficult, to involve families and leaders in decision-making within the school system. The institutionalization of the school as part of the public system generates a potential gap, a vacuum between the school and the community, although community participation is a fundamental element of indigenous education and the permanent evaluation of the teacher and his work.

The relation with the educational system

Another difficulty for the teachers consists in balancing the autonomy of their schools, with regard to decision-making, with the necessity of maintaining relations with the general education system. The government members in charge of supervising, funding and supporting the schools are very badly prepared with regard to the implementation of the new legal and institutional situation. They tend to view the indigenous schools through their occidental models, rather than as a means to stimulate diversity and plurality.

The ambiguity of the situation of indigenous teachers

As a last point, it is important to consider that the issue of intercultural and bilingual education is a complex and ambiguous one, as the indigenous students, teachers, etc., find themselves at a crossroads, asked to choose among different options, which involve not only individual decisions but also a collective and historical responsibility concerning the survival of their languages and cultures. Faced with such a choice, they usually associate dominant non-indigenous technologies, values, knowledge, and national languages with progress and social development. On the contrary, their local language and knowledge is often thought of as, or felt to be, an isolating factor, as merely a vestige of their ancestral cultural past. So it is a daily challenge for them to remain motivated and persevere in their fight for the harmonization of both movements, with a view to strengthening indigenous language and culture, while at the same time valuing, and learning and teaching about, the national and international ones.

The programme has been running since March 1983, **Duration** and its continuity is a priority for the Pro-Indigenous

Commission, for the other indigenous organizations, and for the indigenous peoples themselves.

Funding/Budget

The funds for the programme have come from different sources, in particular from international humanitarian institutions such as OXFAM (1983 – 1990) and the Rain Forest Foundation, Norway (1991 to the present). The indigenous teachers' salaries and the schools' maintenance are the responsibility of the Acrean government, while the training courses, and production of textbooks, are partially supported by the Ministry of Education (in the case of the teacher training) and the Ministry of Environment (the agroforest agent training). Each year the Pro-Indigenous Commission receives around US$200,000.

Responsible organizations and institutions

A great number of organizations are involved in this programme:
The Pro-Indigenous Commission of Acre (CPI/AC)
The Organization of Indigenous Teachers of Acre (OPIAC)
The Association of the Movement of the Agroforest Agents (AMAIAC)
The indigenous local associations of the 12 Nations
The Department of Education of the Acre Government
The Ministry of Education of Brazil
The Ministry of Environment of Brazil

Contacts

Nietta Lindenberg Monte: Educational Adviser
nietta@ism.com.br
Renato Gavazzi, Vera Olinda and Malu Ochoa:
Coordinators for Environment and Education
cpiacre@uol.com.br

BRAZIL:
PRO-YANOMAMI COMMISSION
Sarah Chapple-Sokol and Kate McDermott

Literacy and general education for Yanomami people of all ages

Type of programme and educational level

Seventeen schools in five regions (Demini, Toototobi, Parawau, Homoxi, and Upper Catrimani) within Yanomami territory in Brazil

Geographical and administrative level

Approximately 1,284 Yanomami in Brazil

Indigenous target groups

The Pro-Yanomami Commission (CCPY) began the Yanomami Intercultural Education Project in 1995 to promote literacy in the Yanomae language and in Portuguese. The education programme began in the village of Demini and has subsequently expanded to five different regions. Students are taught literacy in one of the native Yanomami languages (literacy is currently available in three of the four main Yanomami languages), with some going on to learn Portuguese as a second language. Students learn literacy using texts that teach about issues of health, environment, ethno-geography, and ethno-history.[1] The education process allows the Yanomami to have access to information and technical and scientific knowledge about the national society that is necessary

Description of programme

Summary

for the survival of their culture. Furthermore, an applied computer science project has been instituted as a resource for Yanomami teachers and students.

Background: legal-political, socio-economic, educational and linguistic situation

Although a majority of the Yanomami population is still monolingual in a Yanomami language, some of the young people are learning to speak Portuguese in addition to their native tongue (due to greater contact with Brazilian society). In 1992, the territory of the Yanomami in Brazil was legally demarcated. However, their indigenous reserve suffers from recurrent invasions by outsiders, especially ranchers and gold miners. Nevertheless, most Yanomami communities still live according to their traditional subsistence practices of hunting, fishing, shifting cultivation, and gathering. The protection of their lands has become a priority.

General Objectives

Objectives and focus

- To make available to the Yanomami communities the knowledge necessary today to guarantee their rights.
- To strengthen the Yanomami languages so that it is able to absorb and reinterpret new concepts, ideas and words, without weakening the native tongue. (These new concepts, ideas and words originate from contact with the surrounding, Portuguese-speaking, society and are starting to become a part of the day-to-day life of the communities.)
- To promote reflection on the changes that have taken place in Yanomami society since the beginning of contact. [2]

Specific Objectives

- To assure the recognition and financing of the training of teachers and of the schools by the national educational system and, at the same time, make it possible for the Yanomami to appropriate the new intercultural educational process that is being implemented, so that, in the future, they themselves can carry it on.

- To collaborate in the training of Yanomami representatives ('ambassadors'), who can participate in the diverse discussion and decision-making forums that relate to the question of indigenous rights, both in Brazil and abroad.
- To provide support for the training of Yanomami Health Agents.
- To collaborate in the training process necessary (in cartography and in the use of GPS technology, for example) to better prepare the Yanomami to undertake the supervision of their own territory.
- To support initiatives for economic alternatives.[3]

OBJECTIVES FOR APPLIED COMPUTER SCIENCE PROJECT

General objective

- To develop the capacity of the Yanomami teachers to prepare didactic material with the computer.

Specific objectives

- To promote reflection on the editorial preparation of teaching material, considering its function and purpose, and to discuss the diversity of teaching material, its users, costs and production possibilities.
- To introduce the basic concepts of computer science.

- To introduce the use of *Explorer*, *Word*, *PageMaker* and *Photoshop* – the programs currently most used by the Pro-Yanomami staff in the production of teaching material.
- To prepare, along with the students, teaching material: readers, literacy primers, health primers, geography primers, newspapers, etc.
- To prepare a specific primer to teach computer science. [4]

Participation

Community participation is one of the most vital aspects of the programme. Many of the teachers are indigenous, and both teachers and students contribute to creating a curriculum for the schools. Indigenous teachers frequently attend workshops on teaching and developing curriculum. [5] Furthermore, those Yanomami who go on to learn Portuguese in addition to literacy in their native language can participate in defending Yanomami culture and gaining support for it from the larger society. They can then bring back what they have learned to the people in their communities.

Methods used

Teaching and learning takes place through demonstration and discussion, which is reinforced by collaborative and individual exercises and practice. The pedagogy as well as the physical space and materials used are all adapted to the everyday realities of the indigenous communities.

Language of instruction

Students involved in the Yanomami Intercultural Education Project learn in their native language. As native literacy is one of the main goals of the programme, instruction is in the students' mother tongue. Literacy education is currently available in three of the four main Yanomami languages: Yanomae, Yanomam, and Sanum. Although bilingual education in a Yanomami language and in Portuguese was one of the original goals, it has been challenging to establish. Learning Portuguese has proved difficult for the Yanomami, being so isolated from Brazilian society. To learn a second language one must also learn the cultural context of the language. Portuguese includes many concepts that don't exist in traditional Yanomami culture, thereby making it hard for the Yanomami to understand.[6] Thus, the only students who learn Portuguese are those who choose to continue their education so as to become teachers or health workers, and who become in this way 'ambassadors' capable of communicating with the larger society.[7]

Unlike other bilingual-based education programmes, here learning literacy in a Yanomami language is not just a bridge to learning Portuguese. On the contrary, the Yanomami languages are used both in teaching classes and as subjects of study in themselves. Learning literacy in one's native language is just as important here, if not more important, than going on to learn Portuguese.[8]

Curriculum/Themes

The primary goal of the Yanomami Intercultural Education Project, as stated above, is native literacy. Literacy is taught using texts incorporating such subjects as health, environment, ethno-geography, and ethno-history.[9] In teaching Yanomami literacy, it is not only the written form of the language that is taught, but 'traditional indigenous knowledge' is incorporated into the curriculum alongside Brazilian and Western subjects such as basic math skills.[10]

This consequently encourages the use of Yanomami, as opposed to Portuguese, in school. Portuguese is taught to those who will go on to other professions, rather than being a part of the basic curriculum. In some of the Yanomami schools, subjects such as Health Education, Environmental Education, Geography, and Mathematics are being taught.[11]

Teachers attend workshops to learn how to teach and develop curricula themselves. They learn how to teach literacy and mathematics, as well as learning Portuguese as a second language.[12] Besides these skills, teachers get to propose extra subjects of study that will help them in their teaching: at a recent workshop, teachers asked to be taught about money and time, two Western concepts that could help Yanomami in interacting with the national society.[13]

An emerging aspect of the curriculum is applied computer skills. Students learn how to use the computers, which are solar-powered, and teachers use them to create educational materials. Computers are also used to communicate with others in the community, as students and teachers create newsletters for the villages. In addition, computer manuals are being written in the Yanomami languages.

Teachers/Training

Finding qualified teachers for the Yanomami Intercultural Education Project has been a challenge, especially at the outset of the programme. In order for a Brazilian teacher to become involved, he or she not only had to be proficient enough in a Yanomami language to teach literacy in that language, but also had to be knowledgeable about the culture and, furthermore, be willing to live for long periods in the isolated rainforests where the Yanomami live. This obstacle has been largely overcome by the use of indigenous teachers. The latter became a possibility after the first class of students went through the programme and became literate in their native language. They were then able to go further, learning teaching skills and Portuguese, after which they were able to return to their villages to teach. The training of Yanomami teachers is now being carried out in collaboration with the Catholic Diocese of Roraima and other organizations working with the Yanomami: URIHI (Yanomami Health) and SECOYA (Service and Cooperation with the Yanomami People), which works in the regions of Ajuricaba and Marauiá, in the state of Amazonas.

Materials and activities

Blackboards and chalk, and paper and pen/pencil continue to be the primary materials used in the villages, in addition to primers and exercises produced by the Pro-Yanomami staff. Since computers have been introduced into the education programme, teachers and students are beginning to create educational texts and worksheets on the computers for classroom use.

As of late 2001, there were seventeen schools in the five major regions where the Yanomami Intercultural Education Project is established (Demini, Toototobi, Parawau, Homoxi, and Upper Catrimani). A total of 265 students were enrolled in these schools, of whom 120 Yanomami were literate in their native language, and 145 were on the way to being literate. Overall, the education programme has had a significant positive impact on the lives of the Yanomami in the communities that it serves.

Outcomes

Education has allowed the Yanomami to be less dependent on outsiders to defend their land and their human rights. Yanomami who are literate in their native language, or in Portuguese as well, are more prepared and better able to interact with the larger Brazilian society. They can ensure that their land, human rights, traditional culture, and autonomy will not be taken away. Ultimately, this programme will help the Yanomami to maintain their self-sufficient lifestyle, while at the same time allowing them to become teachers, health agents, and 'ambassadors' who will help prevent further dependence upon outsiders.

Lessons learnt: strengths and weaknesses

The programme has operated continuously since its inception in 1995.

Duration

The education programme was initially funded by the Pro-Yanomami Commission (CCPY), with additional support over the years from UNICEF, UNDP, MEC (the Brazilian Ministry of Education and Culture), IWGIA (International Work Group for Indigenous Affairs in Copenhagen), NORAD, OXFAM, Earth Love Fund (England), Survival Gran Canária, OD (Operation one day of work – a collaborative project of Norwegian students)

Funding/Budget

and the Rainforest Foundation of Norway. Most recently, students participating in the Cultural Survival Education Programme (see part B) raised over US$3,500 to purchase computers for Yanomami teachers.

Responsible organizations and institutions

The Pro-Yanomami Commission – CCPY
Fernando Bittencourt (CCPY)
Comissão Pró-Yanomami
SCLN 210 Bloco C sala 209
Brasília – DF – Cep: 70862-530
Telephone/Fax: 61-347-2980
E-mail: proyanomamidf@proyanomami.org.br
Website: http://www.proyanomami.org.br

NOTES:

1. Pro-Yanomami Commission, 2001 http://www.proyano-mami.org.br/frame1/Ingles/educacao.htm
2. Applied Computer Science Project for Yanomami Students
3. http://www.proyanomami.org.br/pei.htm,
   3-4 (accessed 28 July 2003)
4. Applied Computer Science Project for Yanomami Students
5. Yanomami Literacy: Defending Their Land, 4
6. Ibid. 3
7. Ibid.
8. Ibid. 4
9. Pro-Yanomami Commission, 2001 http://www.proyano-mami.org.br/frame1/Ingles/educacao.htm
10. Yanomami Literacy: Defending Their Land, 3
11. Applied Computer Science Project for Yanomami Students
12. Ibid.
13. Yanomami Literacy: Defending Their Land, 4

CAMBODIA: HIGHLAND CHILDREN'S EDUCATION PROJECT (HCEP), RATANAKIRI PROVINCE
CARE International in Cambodia

Multilingual and multicultural primary education combined with pre- and in-service teacher training

Type of programme and educational level

Ratanakiri province, north-east Cambodia, community-governed schools in six villages

Geographical and administrative level

Approximately 800 (48 per cent female) indigenous (Tampuen and Kreung) children and 21 community teachers

Indigenous target group(s)

In a unique co-operation between the Cambodian Ministry of Education, Youth and Sport (MoEYS) and CARE, a three-year pilot project is underway to pilot a model of multilingual, multicultural primary education, delivered in community-governed schools in six remote villages, which have never had any formal or non-formal education before.

Description of programme

Summary

This three-year project provides the first three years of primary education to indigenous children in their own language. Communities have established their own school boards following traditional decision-making processes. Once the schools are operational, the school boards take responsibility for the management of them. The school boards select community teachers, who participate in an intensive teacher training programme. A trained project staff team of indigenous people is supporting these community-based activities. The national curriculum for primary education is being adapted to local conditions, thereby making it relevant to indigenous people. During the three years, a transition will be made to Khmer (the national language) as the primary language of instruction, in order to enable the children to integrate into the government school system.

Background: legal-political, socio-economic, educational and linguistic situation

Ratanakiri province has approximately 100,000 inhabitants. About 65 per cent of the population is indigenous: Tampuen, Jarai and Kreung are the largest ethnic groups in this province. Khmers make up only 25 per cent and are recent immigrants from the lowlands.

Not only are highland minority cultures distinct from mainstream Khmer culture, their languages are distinct as well. With the exception of Jarai, most of the languages belong to the Mon-Khmer group.

The official language in Cambodia is Khmer, a language which most of the indigenous peoples neither speak nor understand. Because the language of instruction in government schools is Khmer and the majority of teachers cannot speak highland minority languages, enrolment and retention rates of indigenous children are the lowest in Cambodia.

The lack of mainstream language skills has made the majority of government schools inaccessible to ethnic minority children. As a result, illiteracy amongst these ethnic minority people is the highest in Cambodia. Amongst the highland minority peoples, only 5.3 per cent of men and less than 1 per cent of women are literate. This is based on a sample of eighty people (thirty-eight men and forty-two women) from a national literacy survey conducted by the MoEYS in co-operation with UNDP and UNESCO (May 2000).

The Highland Children's Education Project aims to address the educational needs of marginalized ethnic minority children. Five interdependent components facilitate the achievement of this goal. The components are:

1. Building a team of ethnic minority resource people to support the establishment and operations of community schools
2. Support for community governance and management of schools
3. Production of culturally appropriate curriculum materials in language, mathematics and socio-cultural studies, adapted from the MoEYS curriculum, in two minority languages
4. Establishment of a stable teaching force of twenty-one community teachers, increasing in competence during the project
5. Linkages with the provincial and national systems of the MoEYS.

Objectives and focus

When surveyed, 98 per cent of families in the six target villages believed that education is important for their children. They also felt that it is important for children to learn about their own culture in school (94 per cent).

Participation

The six school boards have been pivotal in realizing the aim of the project. School board members include traditional village chiefs and elders – highly respected in their communities. The schools were built by the villagers. In one village, each family contributed a woven bamboo panel for the walls.

Having been enabled to establish and manage their own schools, and to select teachers from their own villages, communities are taking ownership of the education of their children for the first time, and in their own language. Community commitment and ownership have resulted in high enrolment and low drop-out rates. In these community schools, the participation of parents and elders is visible: learning also takes place outside the classrooms and parents and elders frequently visit the school.

Methods used

From the beginning, the role of the Highland Children's Education Project was that of an enabling factor for the self-development of indigenous people in the target villages. School boards receive ongoing support and training by indigenous staff members so that they are better able to manage the schools and deal with issues like enrolment, drop-outs and the management of teachers – all new subjects for community members. Nevertheless, the school boards make all decisions, regarding education and schools, independently. Often this is a lengthy process but a more sustainable and worthy one – reinforcing community ownership of and responsibility for the schools and the education of their children.

Language(s) of instruction

The Highland Children's Education Project advocates the use of the highlanders' own language as the initial language of instruction. In the target villages 92 per cent of families felt that it is important for their children to learn to read and write in their own language (Tampuen/ Kreung) but that it is also important for them to learn Khmer (88 per cent). During the three years, a transition will be made to Khmer as the primary language of instruction, in order to enable the children to integrate into the government school system. Indigenous languages have no written form; therefore, the Khmer script has been applied to these languages, incorporating re-instated Khmer letters from the Angkorian period.

In Grade 1, approximately 80 per cent of the instruction is in the students' first language, Kreung or Tampuen. When students begin Grade 2, instruction in and about Khmer will have increased to 40 per cent. To prepare students for a total Khmer Grade 4, 70 per cent of Grade 3 will be taught in Khmer.

While the students' first language and Khmer are not taught at the same time, they can be used at the same time. Teachers use the students' first language to give instructions about Khmer-language activities. They also use it to introduce new Khmer words and expressions and explain what they mean and when they are used. Students use their first language to talk about reading and writing in Khmer. The use of their first language to support the learning of Khmer is an important 'transition to Khmer' strategy. In addition, sociocultural studies is taught in the students' first language.

Curriculum development has been rooted in the daily **Curriculum/Themes** lives of highland minority people. Villagers' knowledge and experience are being used in setting curriculum content and context. This has made the curriculum more accessible and relevant. With local topics being taught, schools become closer to the communities, serving their socio-economic development.

Local topics also contribute to the maintenance and development of traditional culture and lifestyle of ethnic minority groups. The curriculum centres on three subjects: language (Tampuen or Kreung, and Khmer), mathematics and sociocultural studies. HCEP uses the national curriculum of the first three grades of primary education as a model. This is adapted to be more culturally appropriate and written in Kreung and Tampuen languages.

Selecting villages that have never had any form of edu- **Teachers/Training** cation before has meant that the selected community teachers have had little or no formal education. It is important for villages that their teachers come from the village, ensuring the responsibility of the teachers to the community. Therefore, an intensive and extensive teacher-training programme was developed in co-operation with Australia's Batchelor Institute of Indigenous Tertiary Education. Teachers receive an initial six-month pre-service training, which is supported and built upon by a two-year in-service programme. The aim is to upgrade community teachers to a Grade 9 equivalency

and to have them confident and knowledgeable in student-centred teaching and learning.

This methodology is advocated in the MoEYS
'Curriculum for Primary Level', 1996. Action Research
techniques and the Do-Talk-Record methodology are
also incorporated.

The 'student-centred approach' to teaching
requires the teacher to employ a number of teaching
strategies or techniques:

*   Using questions: One of the main aims of primary
    education is to foster intellectual curiosity and a
    desire 'to find out'. Questioning is a basic tool for
    'finding out'.
*   Classroom management: The use of a variety of
    'arrangements of students' allows students to have
    variety of learning interactions, which encourages
    students to be active learners.
*   Using the environment as a teaching resource: The
    use of the environment as a starting point for
    learning enables teachers to contextualize new
    ideas in terms of the students' known environ-
    ment. Elements from the environment become
    teaching and learning material. Teaching starts
    from the known, then moves to the unknown.
*   Using children's mother tongue: Using the chil-
    dren's first language (in this case, the indigenous
    language) brings together the other three techni-
    ques. The teacher facilitates students' exploring of
    their environment in their own words and
    through their own experiences.

Through these techniques, the subject areas of the curriculum are taught, using integrated learning activities
that have a particular subject focus and reflect local
community events and activities.

Materials and activities Since the project is the first to introduce bilingual
schooling in Cambodia, no learning materials existed in

indigenous languages. The materials produced by the project team reflect student-centred methodology. Their colourful appearance and the interesting subjects taken from the children's daily lives make them very appealing to the students. Two basic readers and supplementary teaching materials have been produced. The adaptation of the national curriculum textbooks was slower than expected because of the lengthy revision and formal approval process of the orthography by the MoEYS.

Six school boards (thirty-seven members, of whom thirteen are women) have been established and trained. They were instrumental in establishing, and are now managing, community schools in their village. **Outcomes**

The first cohort of thirteen teachers successfully completed a six-month pre-service training programme. They are now teaching and are receiving in-service training and support at the schools. A new cohort of teachers has been selected.

In February 2003, six community schools opened their doors to 280 students (47 per cent girls). Education has started in villages that never had education before. The average PTR (pupil teacher ratio) is lower than 25:1.

Student materials have been created in two languages: Tampuen and Kreung. The materials consist of two basic readers, some storybooks and supplementary reading material. The adaptation of the MoEYS national textbooks for language and mathematics is under way in both languages.

Research on sociocultural studies has been conducted, and the first chapters for Grade 1 have been developed in three languages (including Khmer).

IMPACT ON WOMEN

In indigenous communities, the workload, especially for women and girls, is very high. Due to the strength of community commitment to education, all the girls that were in the age group for this intake are enrolled in school. Girls make up 47 per cent of the enrolled students. This is markedly higher than the 39 per cent girls' enrolment rate in the government schools (MoEYS statistics 2001 – 2002 for Ratanakiri province).

Only two of the thirteen Community Teachers (15 per cent) are women. One of the criteria to be eligible for training is proficiency in the Khmer language. As we recruited in villages that have never had education before, women who speak Khmer are rather the exception than the rule.

Lessons learnt: strengths and weaknesses

Lack of an Integrated Approach: To come into communities that have never had development opportunities with a single-sector approach to meeting their needs is to ignore the holistic nature of people's needs. For example, concerning the issue of enrolment, one of the responsibilities of children is to carry water from the river to their houses. Since the river is far from the village, children have difficulty arriving at school on time. Community members saw not having a well in the community as an education issue. Though water is not directly an education issue, it has an impact on education. The project has secured funding for wells, which will affect the education and health of children and the community as a whole.

Providing only primary education in remote areas where no education service existed before created problems. Children over twelve years old – as well as adults – need non-formal education in literacy life skills.

Misperceptions of Community Interest: A common belief in the MoEYS and Khmer society is that indigenous people are not interested in education. In fact, the project has demonstrated just the opposite. There is a huge interest in education amongst indigenous people when it is culturally appropriate and meets their needs. In the target villages, there is a huge commitment by the – unpaid – school board members to the schools.

Addressing Community Expectations of Schooling: Working in villages where there has been no experience in formal education has been a complex process. Many parents had the expectation that all of their children could be enrolled, regardless of their age. It was hard to explain why a Pupil Teacher Ratio of 30:1 was better than one of 60:1 when it meant that some children would not be in school. With the school boards, an enrolment schedule was discussed and adopted that permitted the enrolment of all children between ages six and twelve, over the next three years, at an average PTR of 25:1.

School board members show a keen interest in helping to develop the curriculum for the sociocultural studies. Interestingly enough, they not only want ethnic culture in this subject, but also Khmer culture. Just as with the Khmer language, they understand the necessity of their children learning this, if they want to integrate into mainstream Cambodia.

Lack of Trained Indigenous Teachers: Recruiting and training teachers from the remotest villages has meant that candidates have limited or no formal education. Through an extensive training programme and high motivation, teachers have risen to the challenge. At the same time, because they did lack formal schooling, they did not need to be 'de-trained' and then 'retrained' from a traditional teacher-centred classroom. Therefore, a student-centred approach is easier for them to use, and relates better to natural learning. The children are responding very well to student-centred methodology. They are enthusiastic, and absenteeism is low.

Lack of a Curriculum Writer: Adapting national curriculum textbooks is more than translation. The project cannot reasonably expect an expertise from our indigenous staff. The role of a curriculum writer was underestimated in the project design. However, now there is a widespread recognition that such a person is essential, especially for the design of the sociocultural studies curriculum.

Having an Effective Transition Strategy: Several possible strategies have been discussed concerning the community school once the project ends at the end of 2004. Currently we are hoping to extend the project for an additional year so that a full Grade 3 can be completed.

Whatever transition strategy is adopted, the decision will be made with the communities; the schools belong to the community. While the sustainability and integrity of the community schools is the priority, much depends on how the MoEYS will assess the pilot phase. If the evaluation is favourable, a hand-over to the Provincial Office of Education supported by a local NGO would be a possible scenario.

Duration

The three-year project began in January 2002 and concludes in December 2004.

Funding/Budget

The Highland Children's Education Project is being funded by AusAID (the Australian Government's overseas aid program) with additional support from UNICEF and the Canada Fund.

Responsible organizations and institutions

CARE International in Cambodia
Ministry of Education, Youth and Sport, Cambodia
Provincial Office of Education, Ratanakiri Province

Contact

Jan Noorlander and Terry Durnnian
CARE International in Cambodia
E-mail: gabe@care-cambodia.org / care_rtk@camintel.com

We thank Terry Durnnian for revising the draft of this case study.

GUATEMALA: MOBILIZING PROJECT IN SUPPORT OF MAYAN EDUCATION

Katherine Grigsby

Mayan Bilingual and Intercultural Education for Elementary School in forty-eight Local Units of Mayan Education (ULEM)[1] distributed in eight Mayan linguistic regions of Guatemala: Mam, K'iche' Kaqchikel, Tz'utujil, Achi, Q'eqchi, Awakateko and Multilingual

Type of programme and educational level

Geographical and administrative level

10,383 students, of which 5,472 (52.7 per cent) are boys and 4,911 (47.3 per cent) are girls

Indigenous target group(s)

PROMEM (Proyecto Movilizador de Apoyo a la Educación Maya) emerged in a national context characterized by the resurgence of the Mayan Movement in the framework of the democratization and pacification process expressed in the Peace Accords signed in 1996. In this context, specific events occurred of great importance in the life of the nation, such as the formation of the Parity Commission on Education Reform, the First, Second and Third Congresses of Mayan Education, the creation of the National Council of Mayan Education (CNEM), of the Academy of Mayan Languages and of the General Directorate of Bilingual and Intercultural Education (DIGEBI).

Description of programme

Summary

Background: legal-political, socio-economic, educational and linguistic situation

Guatemala is a country with great ethnic, geographical, economic, social, cultural and linguistic diversity. Its population of approximately 11 million is predominantly rural (65 per cent). About 60 per cent are of Mayan origin, concentrated mainly in the rural areas and organized in twenty-one linguistic communities in different regions of the country. Extreme poverty is widespread in the rural areas, affecting approximately 55 per cent of the population, and the Mayan population in particular. The Mayan socio-economic position in society can be characterized in terms of structural marginality and exclusion from basic services. With regard to education, a large proportion of the Mayan population is deprived of school education. Out of 2,322,062 students in the national education system, 806,695 are Mayans and only 24 per cent of them attend Bilingual Intercultural Schools. Likewise, out of 78,272 teachers at the national level, only 18,072 are Mayan, and only 5,976 have been trained in Bilingual Intercultural Education, which represents 33 per cent of the Mayan teachers.

The poor coverage and efficiency of the system are due, however, not only to limited access to school facilities but also to the fact that, historically, the Ladino elite has developed a monocultural and monolingual education system, as they considered education as an instrument for assimilating the Mayan population to the so-called modern Western culture and society. The various expressions of Mayan culture and language were seen as obstacles to development and have been subjected to efforts of elimination through discrimination and racism.

During the years of the project's implementation, Guatemala has progressed in the achievement of an intercultural policy and a policy of generalization of Bilingual and Intercultural Education. The project has been the expression of the decision of UNESCO, the Government and the Netherlands to support the country's democratization processes, the education sector reform, and, particularly, the formulation of a concept and the development of Mayan Bilingual and Intercultural Education, demanded by the Mayan Movement and supported by the Ministry of Education.

PROMEM's vision is based on the recognition of the cultures of peoples as the foundation for national identity and for Guatemalan education. Its aim is to participate in the construction of a multilingual, multicultural and multi-ethnic Guatemalan nation.

Objectives and focus

The objectives of PROMEM are:

- the development of Mayan Bilingual and Intercultural Education
- to support and influence educational reform and national capacity building
- the formulation of a Mayan Bilingual and Intercultural Education proposal based on the ULEMs' best practices
- the training of Mayan teachers for the development and implementation of Mayan Bilingual and Intercultural Education.

Its major components are:

- Mayan Bilingual and Intercultural Education practices in the ULEMs
- Mayan Bilingual and Intercultural curriculum design
- In-service teacher training in Mayan Bilingual and Intercultural Education
- applied research on Mayan culture and language
- systematization of the Mayan Bilingual and Intercultural Education best practices
- editorial and audio-visual production
- a documentation centre.

The project has developed the following strategies:

- emphasis on the quality of interventions and their results
- application of the practice-theory-practice trilogy, in which the beginning and the end of interventions lies in the community, supported by theoretical systematization
- opening of spaces for debate to strengthen the formulation of proposals, with a view to having impact on the educational processes
- construction of alliances with different key players from the civil society at all levels
- innovation in the processes of intervention, and in the educational theories and practices
- participation of parents, teachers, community leaders and authorities in the educational processes
- exchange of innovative experiences and best practices with other schools
- dissemination of progress and results obtained.

Participation

A participatory diagnosis was conducted in each of the linguistic regions where the project would be implemented, with the aim of:

- obtaining the knowledge necessary concerning the socio-economic, cultural and educational reality of their communities
- identifying the educational needs and interests of the communities
- supporting teachers, parents, community members and leaders as well as local education authorities in the formulation of their educational project.

Throughout project implementation, emphasis has been given to developing a broad and active partnership, both inside the system at the central level, and in the schools. Likewise, the collaboration of educational personnel and the community in planning, managing, and implementing the different components of the project has been a priority. A community management approach has been developed in support of the local Mayan education movement that encourages the active participation of parents, women, authorities, local leaders, and other programmes and organizations, generating a synergy of efforts at the local level.

In order to mobilize efforts, initiatives and resources at the local level, the project relies on a group of animateurs under contract with PROMEM who are appointed to the different linguistic communities selected. The animateur's role is to facilitate co-ordination, co-operation and mutual understanding with local authorities, institutions, organizations, programmes and projects; to accompany and provide technical support to the ULEM; and to support local organizations in training activities, management and networking of field activities.

CULTURALLY PERTINENT AND LINGUISTICALLY RELEVANT LEARNING

In response to Guatemala's linguistic and cultural diversity and the discrimination and disadvantages historically faced by the Mayan population with regard to education, the project has emphasized the recovery, valuing, strengthening and promotion of the community's cultural identity as the centre of the educational processes, and on interaction with other communities. In this context, indigenous languages, the world vision, artistic creation, values, traditions, philosophical principles, forms of social organization and spirituality of the Mayan population are conceived as fundamental elements of the learning process. This has been essential for the development of the Mayan children's identity

Methods used

and self-esteem so that they feel proud and enthusiastic about learning.

BUILDING INTERCULTURAL RELATIONS AND LEARNING TO LIVE TOGETHER

Within the framework of national unity, in a multicultural nation like Guatemala, the recognition, respect and valuing of cultural and linguistic diversity by all sectors of society constitutes a major steps towards building intercultural communities. Building intercultural relations and learning to live together in a culturally and diverse society is at the core of the education process in the ULEMs, through:

- recognition of cultural, linguistic and socio-economic diversity
- acknowledgement and valuing of the culture and language of others
- valuing and respecting the identity of each member of a given community
- building a culture of interculturality through education based on four major components: comprehensive development of the human being, life in democracy and a culture of peace, unity in diversity, and all-inclusive sustainable development.

The education process of the ULEMs aims at making children aware of:

- the interaction among different cultures
- that all cultures are creative and genuine expressions of humanity, and that they represent complex and valuable backgrounds of conducts and forms of signification and interpretation of the social and natural reality

- that interculturality not only considers the differences among persons and cultures, but also the similarities among them, their common bonds, shared values, legitimized and accepted norms for living together, and their common interests with regard to local development and national identity, and
- the recognition of the Other as he or she is with his or her codes, capacities, customs and values.

Diverse realities, differentiated strategies

Considering the ULEMs' diverse backgrounds and experiences, the project organized them according to their different levels of progress with regard to Mayan Bilingual and Intercultural Education, resulting in the following categorization according to the Mayan world vision and spirituality:

a)   ULEM Ch'umil (Star, leading light)
b)   ULEM Jotay (Offspring, in development)
c)   ULEM Tikobal (Newborn, promising).

This permitted the development of differentiated training, methodological and pedagogical support, and monitoring and evaluation strategies, according to the specific needs of the ULEMs.

The ULEMs are situated in regions of the country where the Mayan and Spanish languages coexist. Boys and girls speak the indigenous language of their communities, as well as the official Spanish language. Their grandparents and elder members of their communities only speak the indigenous Mayan language, whereas the younger parents are bilingual (Mayan-Spanish). The majority of national schools in their communities teach the indigenous Mayan language in the first two grades of elementary school as a linguistic transition strategy

Language(s) of instruction

towards the official Spanish language. Although most of the teachers are bilingual (Mayan-Spanish), from the third grade onwards they use the indigenous Mayan language for colloquial communication in the classroom, rather than as the language of instruction.

Parents and community members agreed that their children in the ULEMs should be fluent in both their indigenous Mayan language and in the official Spanish language. Therefore, both the indigenous Mayan language of the community and the Spanish language are the official languages of the school.

THE 'NON-NEGOTIABLES' OR ESSENTIAL CRITERIA OF MAYAN BILINGUAL AND INTERCULTURAL EDUCATION

Curriculum/Themes   The project has developed an education proposal that seeks to rescue and revive Mayan culture. It has been important to take ancestral culture and values, as well as the present culture in different regions of Guatemala as a point of departure. This has ensured relevance and a greater identification and commitment at the community level. Likewise, cultural recovery based on reality and on the educational practices developed by the ULEMs has served as the basis for the theoretical construction and development of the content to be incorporated into the curriculum. These are expressed in the 'non-negotiable criteria' or essential elements of Mayan Bilingual and Intercultural Education, which are the following:

- learning and use of two languages: the mother tongue and the official Spanish language
- learning two mathematical systems: the Mayan vigesimal mathematical system and the Western decimal mathematical system
- learning and experiencing a complementary

system of values: the indigenous Mayan values and universal values

- learning about the different Mayan indigenous art expressions and those of the different cultures of the country and the world
- learning to identify, analyse and interpret the world based on the Mayan indigenous culture and on the knowledge universally accumulated by humanity.

The classroom curriculum and pedagogical practices:

- are based on a new meaning of content, understood as the learning of concepts, procedures, attitudes and values, characteristic of the culture to which the children belong.
- place the trilogy student – learning – teacher in the centre of the curriculum.
- emphasize significant learning according to the constructivist learning theory, that is, the construction of significant knowledge as the nucleus of the teaching-learning process, through which children learn concepts, procedures, attitudes and values when they can attribute meaning to them.
- take into account that the attribution of meaning to knowledge depends on the capacity of the child to establish substantive relations between what is new and what he/she already knows, that is to say, between new knowledge and previous knowledge, a process in which his/her culture and mother tongue play a determining role. The achievement of this is mediated by the child's interaction with his/her culture: concepts, explanations, reasoning, language, ideology, customs, values, beliefs, feelings, interests, attitudes, norms, family, economic and social organization.
- assume that the relation between the methodology of teaching (the teacher) and the learning results (the children) is mediated by the prioritization

of the child's processes of construction of knowledge.

- are based on the articulation between culture – learning – education – school content, through which 'any element of the culture of a given social group which it considers should be integrated by its members can be converted into contents of teaching' (C. Coll).
- consider the areas of knowledge contained in indigenous Mayan language, mathematics, values, and art as being the foundations of the indigenous Maya culture, and assign them their proper place in the curriculum, namely, as (appropriate) subjects of learning and teaching in the national education system.
- are oriented to the development of competencies, which are understood as complex capacities (with different degrees of integration) that are manifested in the different dimensions of human life. The competencies are understood as expressing different degrees of personal development and of participation in social processes, and as constituting a synthesis of lived human experience.

Materials and activities   The project provides the ULEMs with basic education materials, which in turn are used by teachers to develop their own. These include: bilingual textbooks, children's reading books in Mayan languages, Mayan educational games, Mayan musical instruments (marimbas and *chinchines*), cotton yarn for weaving Mayan textiles, Mayan calendars, Mayan glyphs.

Among the main activities promoted are:

Pedagogical Projects

These take into account the knowledge that students already have. Teachers and students choose a theme or topic and formulate questions according to their interests and context. Together they establish the strategies and decide how do they want to implement it. Parents and community members take active part in it as resource persons. Its implementation requires that the teacher play the role of a facilitator. Likewise, the ULEM or the school is not the only place where the students learn, since according to the interests and needs, new learning spaces are chosen, such as farms, rivers, archaeological sites and different community institutions. Pedagogical Projects imply active and participative learning strategies and they require a systematic recording of the findings, the information and the knowledge produced by the students.

Learning Centres or Learning Corners

Teachers and students collect a variety of local materials to be used in the learning process, such as the sand table used in writing exercises, as well as seeds, sticks, leaves, stones and other materials used in mathematics as well as in science learning. These materials are combined with books, magazines, newspapers, journals, maps, drawings, music and videotapes, complemented by the students' projects.

Musical and Artistic Groups

Parents or community musicians teach students to play Mayan instruments such as the Marimba. Likewise, with the active involvement of artistic community groups they learn dances and theatre plays, which they prepare and present on special occasions according to the Mayan calendar.

Teachers/Training

No process of change can occur without the committed participation of well-trained teachers. In the case of Mayan Bilingual and Intercultural Education, this is particularly true due to the following factors: (a) the lack of Mayan teachers, (b) the loss of the mother tongue in many Mayan teachers, (c) the reduced number of Mayan teachers who have mastered the writing of their mother tongue, and (d) the insufficient training options offered by the State in Bilingual Intercultural Education.

Consequently, the project implements four programmes:

a) in-service training of ULEM teachers
b) training of animators of Mayan Bilingual and Intercultural Education
c) specialization in Mayan Bilingual Intercultural Education and Curriculum (academic course)
d) Bachelor's Degree in Bilingual Intercultural Education.

Both the in-service teacher training and the training of animators have been an important effort appreciated by directors and teachers. The impact in the learning process is significant, particularly with regard to the teaching-learning process of the five 'non-negotiable' or essential criteria of Mayan Bilingual and Intercultural Education, the cultural and linguistic relevance of the learning environment, and the use of active and participatory methodologies and co-operative work.

The Specialization programme in Mayan Bilingual Intercultural Education and Curriculum is aimed at providing teachers with the knowledge and competence required in a bilingual and intercultural learning situation. One of its main characteristics is that its content is organized around issues considered by teachers as fundamental, based on their own teaching experience. Emphasis is made in applied research and systematization. Teachers participating in the programme feel satisfied with the results and are extremely motivated to continue their studies to earn a higher teaching degree and/or a university degree.

The Bachelor's degree programme in Bilingual

Intercultural Education is aimed at professors of teacher-training schools. It is an interesting model that aims to provide the knowledge and competence required in the training of elementary school teachers in Mayan Bilingual and Intercultural Education. The programme has been successful in the use of active methodologies to promote creativity; co-operative work; reflection and debate; the systematic study of Mayan culture and language; and the design of pedagogical projects based on the need to change and improve educational practices in both teacher training schools and elementary schools, by taking into consideration the students' culture and language.

Outcomes

• Mayan Culture and Language is now beginning to be perceived as an essential component of national education and as a major contribution to the multicultural, multilingual and multi-ethnic configuration of the Guatemalan nation. Thus, Mayan Bilingual and Intercultural Education seems to have gained acceptance from large sectors of society.

• Applied research may have an invaluable impact on the education process and its development, particularly the studies on the ways in which Mayan children learn and on the forms of Mayan organization. In methodological terms, it constitutes a contribution to classroom educational practices both in Mayan Bilingual and Intercultural Education schools and in the whole education system.

• The combination of applied research, Mayan Bilingual Intercultural curriculum and pedagogical practices, and teacher-training programmes has been a successful strategy that constitutes a significant contribution to education reform and curricular transformation.

• Although the level of development of Mayan Bilingual and Intercultural Education in the individual

ULEMs varies, in general terms, the latter have shown significant achievements in the affirmation of culture and language in the learning process.

- Likewise (though it is too soon to fully assess), the practice of cultural values, the use of indigenous language, and the practice of intercultural relations and democracy in the ULEMs has had a positive influence on school directors, teachers, students and community members. One of the most important achievements is the reaffirmation, strengthening and development of self-identity and self-esteem in children, who now feel enthusiastic about learning.

- ULEMs' grade repetition and drop-out rates are lower than that of the monolingual national schools, where most children are of Mayan origin.

- The training programmes have had a positive effect in improving the teaching-learning process and its results.

Lessons learnt: strengths and weaknesses

- The processes developed by the project are promising, but they are not yet sufficiently consolidated. The generalization of Mayan Bilingual and Intercultural Education in the areas where the majority of Mayan indigenous population is concentrated is a task that should not be postponed, but attended to, by the State (in particular the Ministry of Education), the society, and the Mayan organizations, with the support of international co-operation.

- The implementation of a genuinely intercultural national curriculum is under way. The achievements of the project will only be consolidated to the extent that Mayan Bilingual and Intercultural Education is incorporated into education reform, curriculum transformation, teacher-training programmes and national education legislation.

- Mayan Bilingual and Intercultural Education in

general has not yet spread to surrounding schools, due mainly to a certain dispersion of the ULEMs and to the lack of co-ordination with provincial education directorates. There is a need, then, to establish school networks as a mechanism of promoting and spreading best practices in the geographical areas where the most advanced ULEM (Ch'umil) are located.

- Among the most pressing tasks are greater methodological and curriculum development of scientific contents of Mayan culture, the design and implementation of pedagogical projects combined with productive components, and the search for and negotiation of alternatives to ensure sustainability of the ULEMs, especially the community education centres.

- The teacher-training programmes should be developed further to achieve greater levels of relevance and to strengthen Mayan Bilingual and Intercultural Education. Specific training programmes for school directors and women have not yet been realized.

1 July 1999 to 31 December 2003

Duration

US$3,890,598

Funding/Budget

UNESCO Office for Central America

Responsible organization(s)

Katherine Grigsby
Chief Technical Advisor PROMEM
UNESCO Guatemala
4a. Calle 1-57. Zona 10.
Ciudad de Guatemala
Guatemala 01010
Tel: + 502 360 8040, 360 8034
Fax: + 502 331 1524
E-mail: k.grigsby@unesco.org

Contact

NOTE:

1. Twenty-two ULEMs correspond to Mayan community education centres; fourteen to PRONADE, a Ministry of Education programme which supports educational self-management in rural communities; and eight to the Ministry of Education Bilingual and Intercultural Education Programme.

INDIA: CHAKMA LANGUAGE PRESERVATION PROJECT

Suhas Chakma

Introduction of indigenous language as subject in formal primary schools

Type of programme and educational level

Chakma Autonomous District Council (CADC) Kamlanagar, Chawngte district, Mizoram, India

Geographical and administrative level

Chakma children under the Chakma Autonomous District Council

Indigenous target group(s)

In its effort to preserve the language and the scripts, the Chakma Autonomous District Council (CADC) of Mizoram introduced the Chakma Language as a subject of the curriculum in the eighty-five primary schools run by the CADC in 1997. The CADC was established pursuant to the 6th Schedule of the Constitution of India in 1972. It has powers over primary education.

Description of programme

Summary

   This project provides the Chakma children the opportunity to learn the Chakma language and at the same time obtain general education in accordance with the Mizoram State Education Board. The teachers opting for the Chakma language have to undergo training programmes both in the Chakma language and other languages required to teach the subjects recommended by the School Education Board. The main aim of the project is to preserve the Chakma script and develop it for teaching in high schools. Despite its weaknesses, the project has been successful.

Background: legal-political, socio-economic, educational and linguistic situation

In 1900, Chittagong Hill Tracts (CHTs) was divided and a portion of it was included under then Lushai Hills (now Mizoram). After Indian Independence in 1947, Lushai Hills as a part of Assam also became a part of India. The Chakma Autonomous District Council is situated in the Chawngte district of the Indian State of Mizoram.

The Chakmas faced and continue to face serious discrimination from the majority Mizos. The Chakmas allege that the Government of Mizoram has always followed a policy of denial and deprivation against the Chakmas. Consequently, the Chakmas have remained deplorably behind development in all respects, as indicated by the following statistics:

- *Education*: After enjoying fifty years of independence, the majority of the Chakmas still do not have access to education. The general literacy percentage may not be more than 15 per cent, while female literacy is less than 1 per cent. This despite the fact that the Mizoram State has the highest literacy rates in India. This illiteracy is not due to Chakmas not wanting to be literate, nor to lack of merit or intelligence, but rather due to the fact that the Chakmas have all along been deprived of any facilities for pursuing education. Only in recent years have a few middle and high schools and a college been established in Chakma areas by the CADC. However, these educational institutions have no assistance, financial or otherwise, from the Mizoram State Government. Even now very few Chakma students can attend any government educational institution within the state of Mizoram, owing to harassment and physical torture.

- *Employment*: According to the 1994 census report of Government employees published by the Directorate of Economics and Statistics, Mizoram, Aizawl, there are 40,420 employees of the Government of Mizoram. Yet, of these, there are only 240 Chakma employees. Of these, there are only two Gazetted Officers, while all the others are employed in the C & D categories (i.e. non-gazetted officers). This is clear evidence of discrimination as regards employment opportunities. Under the Government rules, education in Mizo language up to Class VI is compulsory. Since most of the Chakmas do not speak Mizo language, they are completely denied employment opportunities.
- *Development Activities*: Most of the Chakma-inhabited areas do not have basic infrastructural facilities. For example, there are no roads in these areas, nor has there been any substantive developmental activity.

Preservation of the script

Objectives and focus

Apart from the Chakma Autonomous District Council in Mizoram, there is no constitutionally recognized body for the Chakmas anywhere in the world. Consequently, before the District Council began this programme, the Chakmas were unable to learn, teach and preserve the language.

Although the Chakmas are one of the few groups of indigenous peoples in South Asia having their own script, the Chakma script has become nearly extinct. It would not be an overstatement to say that 99.9 per cent of the Chakmas are unable to read it. It was for these reasons that the preservation of the Chakma script was one of the main priorities of the CADC.

Cultural development
Learning in the Chakma language will develop cultural identity of the Chakma students and help them to relate to with other Chakmas all over the world.

Participation

The CADC has an elected local parliament. Elections to the CADC are conducted by the State Election Commission. The project has been a long standing demand of the Chakmas and its introduction has been welcomed by all Chakmas as there is no other way to preserve the Chakma script.

Methods used

The methods of teachings are formal:

- introduction of learning in the Chakma language as a compulsory subject in primary schools
- classroom teaching
- homework, assignments and essay writing
- classroom examination
- board examination.

Languages of instruction

In the eighty-five primary schools run by the CADC, the medium of instruction is English. Students can choose a modern Indian language, e.g. Hindi or Mizo. The Chakma language is only one subject of the curriculum.

Curriculum/Themes

Pattam Paida (first step): consists of introduction of script and grammar

Di Paida (second step): grammar and stories

Teachers/Training

The teachers opting for the Chakma language have to undergo training programmes both in the Chakma language and other languages required to teach the subjects recommended by the School Education Board. All the teachers teaching Chakma are Chakmas themselves. A few elderly persons preserve the Chakma script as it is required for traditional healing, and so on. A few learn it by themselves. There is a lack of trained teachers in Chakma language, a situation that is currently being redressed through a teacher-training programme.

Materials and activities

Although efforts are being made to develop software for the Chakma script, there is no computerized or machine-made script for the Chakma language. Consequently, publication of the textbooks faces problems of circulation. A Chakma student at the Indian Institute of Technology and a few software engineers are developing the software for the script. A sample of the Chakma script can found at http://www.alphabets-world.com/chakma.html.

Positive Outcomes

During these six years as many as 700 Chakma students have completed their primary education in the Chakma language and a corresponding number are studying in each grade ranging from pre-school to Sixth Grade. For the first time in a long time, a large number of Chakmas communicate through their own language. This is a milestone for the preservation of the Chakma script.

Outcomes

Lessons learnt: strengths and weaknesses

The success of the programme has been impressive. A recent record reveals that nearly 10 per cent of the total Chakma student population have gained proficiency in reading and writing their language. A growth in literary activities in the Chakma language is becoming apparent. The achievement has been encouraging, and the enthusiasm of Chakmas for learning to read and write their own language has grown.

Weaknesses of the programme

Lack of resources
The programme has been suffering from a lack of resources as there is no grant from the government of India, or the State government of Mizoram, to develop the language.

*Lack of trained teachers*There is a lack of trained teachers in the Chakma language although many teachers are being trained presently.

Lack of computerized script
Although efforts are on the way to develop software for the Chakma script, there is no computerized or machine-made script for the Chakma language. Consequently, publication of the textbooks faces problems of circulation.

Duration

The project started in 1997 and is ongoing.

Funding/Budget

There are no resources from the Mizoram State government.

Responsible institution(s)

Contact

Mr Suhas Chakma
Asian Indigenous and Tribal Peoples Network
P.O. Box 9627C-2/78, Janakpuri
New Delhi 110058
IndiaTel: + 91 11 25620583, 25503624
Fax: + 91-11-25620583
E-mail: aitpn@aitpn.org

MALAYSIA: SNAKE AND LADDER PROJECT IN SABAH

Jannie Lasimbang, PACOS TRUST

Early Childcare and Development (ECD) for pre-school indigenous children aged from 4 to 6 years

Type of programme and educational level

Thirteen ECD community centres co-ordinated by PACOS TRUST (hereafter referred to as PACOS) in ten districts throughout Sabah, namely Suausindak, Kipouvo, Togudon and Terian in the Penampang District; Tiga in the Tambunan District; Kalampun in the Keningau District; Tinangol in the Kudat District; Liu Tamu and Kodong in the Pitas District; Kuamut in the Kinabatangan District; Gana in the Kota Marudu District, and Tiong in the Tuaran District

Geographical and administrative level

Kadazandusun, Rungus, Murut, Sonsogon and Sungai

Indigenous target group(s)

The project is part of the PACOS' Community Education (COMED) Programme that focuses on indigenous children preparing to enter government primary schools. The ECD project provides basic to advanced training for indigenous pre-school teachers so that they can undertake the running of community ECD centres. It also constantly refines a curriculum incorporating the indigenous way of life that suits the needs and aspirations of

Description of programme

Summary

communities, while linking the curriculum to the official education curriculum of the government, so that the students can meet the government academic standards for entering primary one. Other programmes by PACOS – such as the Community Organising and Training Programme, Land Rights and Resource Management, and the Socio-Economic Programmes in the different villages in which the ECD centres are found – also support the pre-school.

Background: legal-political, socio-economic, educational and linguistic situation

In 1993, PACOS started its first ECD pilot project among the Kadazandusun community in the kampong (village) Kipouvo, Penampang with financial support from the Bernard van Leer Foundation, the Netherlands. Being the first school, it tended to follow the curriculum set by other conventional pre-schools because of a lack of experience of the teachers from the community and of the programme co-ordinator. However, traditional songs, stories and the use of the vernacular language were all introduced as part of the subjects. When two other ECD centres were opened in the same year, the teachers were able to come together to discuss incorporating further aspects of the indigenous way of life in the school.

The management committee of PACOS, however, had always conceptualized the ECD as a way of immersing young pre-school children in indigenous systems, so that they will have a strong foundation when entering formal schooling and may need to be separated from their communities.

The need to separate from their community life and customary land in order to attend school, and the need to be inculcated with a euro-centric education system, have been identified by many indigenous communities as key causes of the erosion of indigenous knowledge and of the declining appreciation of indigenous systems among younger generations. In 1998, PACOS decided to establish Suausindak, an ECD centre in the Penampang district, where indigenous pre-school teachers are trained. Suausindak also formed a core group to develop a curriculum that will incorporate aspects of indigenous systems and ways of life.

- *Revitalization of appreciation of indigenous systems by incorporation into the ECD curriculum*

  Indigenous systems are based on harmony between the community and the immediate environment. Importance is placed on respect for community pride and on the maintenance of the integrity of the natural resource base. For indigenous communities, these systems have safeguarded and established a peaceful coexistence, a sustainable livelihood and use of resources. Much of the knowledge and practice of indigenous systems have been lost or denigrated due to lack of acceptance of a pluralistic system by governments and society, and to the pursuit of wealth in the present capitalist economy. This objective of the community ECD project is therefore an attempt to revitalize the appreciation by indigenous children of their culture through incorporating aspects of indigenous systems in the curriculum.

- *Multilingualism*

  Language carries with it the cultures and knowledge of a people. In all government schools in Sabah, only the Malay language is used, with English as one of the subjects. The introduction of the Kadazandusun language is very recent and is still limited to a few primary schools. With strong pressure to prepare children to speak Malay in schools, parents have started to use Malay at home. As such, the vernacular language is slowly dying. The project, therefore, also aims at strengthening the use of vernacular language in the ECD centres. Also, given the increasing interaction between the thirty-nine ethnic groups in

Sabah, the project tries to introduce songs and other activities in other indigenous languages, with the hope that this will help foster understanding and harmony between groups.

- *Academic achievement*
  Many schools in the rural areas have low academic achievements and high drop-out rates. The causes for this are many, but chief among them are the low standards of the education facilities and the lack of commitment of teachers who have been assigned to rural schools. By training community pre-school teachers who are committed, and assisting community organizations who can work with primary schools to improve such standards, it is hoped that indigenous children will have a better chance to succeed as they progress from pre-schools to primary schools.

Participation

PACOS insists that the establishment of an ECD centre in an indigenous community be endorsed by, and receive full support from, the community. Thus, before a centre is set up, a community meeting has to be held to discuss the project, get the consent of the whole community, identify potential teacher(s) from the community, and do a survey on the number of children aged 4 – 6 years. The curriculum, as well as the contribution of the community, will also be discussed in detail and agreed upon. A community ECD committee will then be established to oversee the project. Thereafter, the teacher(s) will undergo training, while the ECD committee will visit nearby indigenous ECD centres in order to learn from their experiences. PACOS in the meantime will seek funding support for the community ECD, after identifying the contributions and needs of the community, such as fees, donations for food, building and teaching aids.

Methods used

What sets the community ECD centres apart from other pre-schools in the country, which mainly focus on academic achievement, is the use of a thematic concept, interaction and community involvement.

Indigenous Thematic Concept

Curriculum development has evolved towards using indigenous thematic concepts that run throughout the subjects taught at the community ECD centres. Although much is needed to improve the themes to reflect much more about indigenous systems, it has already reached a stage where indigenous children can learn about their traditional way of life, in a way that is linked to their immediate environment and community. The building up of the themes from one level to another ensures continuity and a stronger grasp by the children of the systems.

Interaction

Direct interaction between teachers and students, and between students and the community, is encouraged. Interaction between the lessons learned in class and real life experience are also stressed. The immediate physical environment is used to make subjects alive. If a primary school exists in the community, joint dialogues are organized to encourage educators to incorporate aspects of indigenous systems – such as the resource management system that respects the harmony between people and nature, a social system that is based on good behavioural conduct, and an economic system based on the principles of reciprocity, social responsibility and sustainability – into the formal curriculum or into their co-curriculum activities, as well as to improve the overall standards of the primary school.

Community Involvement

The community ECD centre is considered by PACOS as one of the principal starting points for any participatory community education project and as a tool for community organizing. As such, the community is made to understand, from the very beginning, the necessity of its involvement in the ECD project. Teachers are selected by the community, with advice from the PACOS ECD Programme Coordinator and other staff involved in the area. All the teachers in the current thirteen ECD centres are women. Each teacher is given at least six months training at the Suausindak ECD training facility and teaching practice in an established community ECD centre. After the training, the teacher will start teaching in her or his own community, but with supervision by the PACOS monitoring unit, made up of teachers and community organizers. The community through the elected ECD committee are also expected to guide the teacher and provide supervision.

The community usually contributes resources such as food, drinks, and locally available teaching aids such as seeds, fruits and samples of medicinal plants. When the pre-school compound needs to be beautified, a *gotong royong*, or communal labour contribution, will be organized. Often the teachers seek help by asking for stories, songs, riddles, and so on, and sometimes the elders are called upon to come to the school as storytellers. In some communities where they have started a traditional medicine garden, the children are brought there to learn about herbs and medicinal plants. This, however, is very much dependent on the creativity of the teacher.

Each month, a meeting is organized by the Community Organization where the ECD committee is expected to update and discuss the progress of the centre. Problems are first brought up at the ECD committee meetings, but if deemed serious enough they will be discussed at the community meetings and with the PACOS Management Committee.

Books, Tapes and Performances
To popularize the programme and to increase the availability of teaching aids, the ECD centres may produce their own books and music cassettes or collaborate with other organizations, such as the Bernard van Leer

Foundation and the Kadazandusun Language Foundation. The centres also accept offers for children to perform traditional songs, dances, etc., in important events. As much as possible, events will be organized by the ECD centre itself in order to provide the students and teachers opportunities to popularize traditional songs, music and dances, as well songs in the vernacular language.

All the centres are encouraged to provide the children with a good base in their mother tongue but at the same time, they are taught to be multilingual, depending on the capability of the community and the teacher(s). The main languages are the vernacular and Malay, but English may also be taught as a subject. Students are also encouraged to learn traditional songs from other communities, as this will help the children in future interactions.

Language(s) of instruction

PACOS first started to develop a curriculum based on themes that highlight indigenous ways of life in 1996. The first effort to try and build upon the individual experiences of the teachers was through a collaboration with the Kadazandusun Language Foundation (KLF) to produce a language workbook for children from five to six years of age. It took the team a whole year to work on the ten selected themes, and finally the book was published in 2001. The themes revolved around the child ('Me') and the environment ('My House', 'Occupation/Work', 'Animals', 'Festivals', 'Fruits', 'Vehicles', 'Useful Plants', 'Vegetables' and 'Water'). Community pre-school teachers and Suausindak shared their experience from teaching children the curriculum incorporating traditional life. Inspiration and experiences were also drawn from other organizations working with children, such as Chetna and organizations working with support from the Bernard van Leer Foundation.

Curriculum/Themes

The production of the book allowed other communities to have a rough guide for their monthly themes in 2002. Each teacher had to develop their own lesson activities and lesson plans. For those communities who do not speak the Kadazandusun language, they have an extra burden, as they need to find or elaborate material in their own language. Interviews with community pre-school teachers have shown that the daily activities varied considerably, depending on whether teachers are knowledgeable in the subjects and whether they can solicit help from elders in the community. In general, however, teachers managed to find traditional activities for their lessons.

To develop a more comprehensive curriculum incorporating indigenous systems, a team was formed comprising experienced teachers of Suausindak. Current work on the curriculum also includes efforts to integrate it with the national curriculum, for the rules are tightening concerning pre-school facilities to ensure that the national curriculum is used as a guideline. The Suausindak core of teachers, however, are now preoccupied with how to provide for the immediate need for a more detailed activity and taking the themes from one age group to the next, rather than delving deeper into indigenizing the themes further, although some changes were also made in those directions.

Teachers/Training

The PACOS COMED programme now has a total of twenty-four community pre-school teachers or aides and six people at the co-ordination level. Among the most difficult tasks in designing such a curriculum is making community ECD aides understand the curriculum itself. Most teachers have not had formal education, which has posed a challenge for the core group in explaining the contents. Because of the rigid nature of formal schooling which the pre-schools facilitated by PACOS follows, it is difficult to hold regular meetings among teachers. The bimonthly joint tactic session for PACOS staff and community representatives provided the space, but the teachers still found it difficult to approach the supervisors in Suausindak because they too had their own teaching period. Some admitted that the culture of not asking questions or sharing is something they found difficult to overcome. Realizing the need for confidence-building, many of the teachers who could be spared were sent for training courses and exposure to other schools. Teachers were also made aware, and now accept, that the monitoring activities are meant to assist them rather than to find faults.

The PACOS ECD centres operate as individual entities – materials and activities are produced by the teachers with help from the community. The Programme Co-ordinator and her team provide a rough guideline on the subjects and themes, but each lesson plan will have to be decided and developed by the teachers themselves. The centre is usually a building that already exists in the community, for example the community hall. However some communities have built their own ECD centre from their own contributions or with the help of other donors facilitated by PACOS (e.g. the Inner Wheel Club).

Materials and activities

In 1998, PACOS decided to establish Suausindak, an ECD centre in the Penampang district, where teachers are trained. Suausindak is also a comprehensive pre-school with its own classes for pre-school children up to six years old, computer lab, resource centre, and a place where all the community ECD teachers can come and meet and learn. Since most of the experienced teachers are stationed in Suausindak, a core group was formed to prepare guidelines on the themes and lesson plans for community ECDs. Teachers from these centres also participate in the preparation of the guidelines.

As much as possible, the community ECD centres get their supplies for the teaching aids from the surroundings. Food and other resources needed for the pre-school lessons and building are also contributed by the community from their own gardens and forest. However, other materials are bought from nearby towns or from PACOS.

Impact on Pre-school Children

Outcomes

Indigenous children generally enjoy a lot of freedom – to follow adults or play with other children. They may also be given specific chores. Whether following adults or doing their chores, they are taught all the time about many important things in life. This makes the indigenous education system part of living. There is no distinction between working and playing. For example, among the favourite pastimes of children is to go to the river with friends to fish – and in the process learn an important skill for survival. From a young age, children take part in all domestic activities such as caring for their younger siblings.

For children who are now attending the ECD centres, life has not changed dramatically. They appear to have made school part of their daily lives. The beauty of the community ECD centres is that they are located within the villages and, more importantly, the children are within the parents' reach. They go to school, and then can be part of the domestic and family life after school finishes.

Impact on the Community

For the community, the ECD has been a source of learning in many ways. In the early part of the project, some members of the community were opposed to teaching the vernacular language in the pre-school, as they felt that the children speak this at home, and they wanted instead for their children to be taught in Malay so that they will be better prepared when they go to primary school. After a lot of convincing, they now see the importance of inculcating the use of the language and understanding of culture, tradition and indigenous knowledge up to the age of six years. Parents are now showing pride in their children's ability to speak their language and knowledge of their culture. It also made the community realize that passing knowledge to the next generation through the ECD centre is important and will need their input to develop a relevant curriculum.

Working with and in the ECD centres in their communities also provided the teachers and leaders an opportunity to improve themselves. Since most of the teachers and community ECD committee members are women, it encouraged them to be active, committed and organized, to make decisions and interact with other leaders and teachers from other communities.

The negative aspect of the centre is the increasing dependence of the community on the teachers for the education of the children. Traditionally, every adult in the community is expected to take care of the education of children. Through examples, each member of the community plays an important role in equipping the young with relevant knowledge and skills required to lead an independent life. Knowledge may be transmitted through a process of apprenticeship; the practice of the oral tradition; direct observation and instruction; and through dreams, natural talents or divine gifts.

Interest in Culture vs.
Immediate Environment Providing the Culture

Besides PACOS, some other pre-schools in rural Sabah have also been working to incorporate local cultures in their school curriculum. It is uncertain whether these initiatives are driven by an effort to make the lessons understood by using activities in the immediate environment to give students a more visual impact, or by a genuine interest in indigenous peoples' way of life. The reason is therefore part of the issue. If indeed there is a genuine move towards incorporating indigenous systems into the curriculum, then the subsequent concern is the lack of understanding about indigenous systems.

Lessons learnt: strengths and weaknesses

This has made PACOS more conscious of the need for the community ECD centres and its teachers to be aware of this distinction.

The Teacher's Limitations

Despite the interest, one of the main problems is how curriculum developers limit the understanding of indigenous systems to cultural expressions. Children are taught traditional dances, music, songs, languages and even traditional medicines or agricultural activities.

The issue, therefore, is not the lack of what can be taught, but the young caregivers' lack of knowledge about indigenous systems, the way of life, ceremonies, cosmology, and so on, and how this lack of knowledge affects their ability to embed activities and subjects in indigenous spirituality and concepts. There is also still a lack of discussion on how to introduce these as lessons suitable for pre-school children. Below are illustrations of this issue:

A pre-school teacher was asked about the kind of activities that she teaches, and she gave 'birthdays' as an example. To incorporate this in the lessons on Mathematics and Morals, she uses the age and the number of candles on the birthday cake to teach about numbers, and the sharing of the cake and inviting other children for a birthday to illustrate important values. In studying indigenous cultures, however, birthdays ceremonies (momuga) would have made a poor topic because birthdays are seldom celebrated and certainly not in the way described (with cakes and parties).

For the theme on the environment/universe, ready-made Western books on the stars and constellations are often used. However, indigenous peoples have their own way of recognizing the stars and the galaxy, of forecasting the weather and using the moon to guide planting seasons.

Strategizing and Planning

Developing a comprehensive curriculum incorporating indigenous concepts is a lengthy process involving constant practice and subsequent review. However, there is a need for a clear policy towards full incorporation. This would guide curriculum developers to identify themes and subsequently hold discussions to fully explore suitable aspects of indigenous life that would fit into activities and lesson plans for relevant age groups. For PACOS, such discussions need not start from scratch as the information gathered by other programmes on indigenous systems can already be a good source.

Whose Culture?

In a multi-ethnic community like Sabah, it is important to make a policy for the community pre-schools. Although use of language is quite clear, it is important to clarify that each pre-school will only be guided by a set of ideas and that every community can identify their own tradition to coincide with the theme, activities and lesson plans. This would in fact be a strength for PACOS' pre-schools which have already started on lessons and some of the cultural aspects of the different communities. The task would also present an opportunity to community pre-school committees for active participation.

Challenges:
Revitalizing Indigenous Education System

Traditionally, the children are taught by everyone in the community. A child grows up with the guidance of the whole community and learns through direct observation and involvement, from a young age imitating adults, or be allowed to use, and thus familiarize themselves with, tools such as the *parang* (a sort of chopper or long knife, made by local blacksmiths).

By the age of 12, the child is competent to do an adult's work. For example, parents would bring along their children to work in the farm and teach them what they need to learn about things that are appropriate for their age. Through examples from the adults around them, children learn their *adat*, which entails knowing how one ought to live in a community. Children also learn, at an early age, certain prohibitions and limitations of what one can do in a community. Knowledge is also acquired through oral tradition, through repeated information, continued practice and practice/action with reflection.

Ultimately, it is very important for PACOS to reflect how far it wants to go as far as revitalizing indigenous education system. At present, the various ECD centres are trying a balance that conforms with the national education policy for all pre-schools in Malaysia but incorporates indigenous systems into its own curriculum. Whether this will continue in the future or be curtailed by the Government is unsure. The other question is whether the PACOS ECD project should be satisfied with its present work, that is, with accepting that adaptation to both worlds is inevitable, or whether it will it go on to reconstruct a situation that promotes an indigenous education system.

Duration

Support from the Bernard van Leer Foundation started in 1993, renewable on a three-year project period. It is hoped that the project will be for the long term. After a certain period, the community ECD centres would take the responsibility of financing part of the centre (or the whole project if community resources allows).

Funding/Budget

Each centre runs on a minimum budget of Malaysian Ringgit 450 per month, or RM5,400 per year (US$1,422), which includes allowances for the teacher, teaching aids and food. The community supplements this with local contributions in the form of school fees, food and labour.

PACOS Trust, Sabah

Anne Lasimbang
Co-ordinator, Community Education Programme
P.O. Box 511, 89507 Penampang, Sabah, Malaysia
Tel: (60-88) 712518 (PACOS TRUST), (60-88) 729067
(Suausindak)
Fax: (60-88) 718669
E-mail: pacos@tm.net.my
Website: http://www.sabah.net.my/PACOS

**Responsible
organization(s)**

Contact

MEXICO:
THE BILINGUAL AND INTERCULTURAL TELESECUNDARIA
'JUAN FRANCISCO LUCAS',
OF SAN ANDRES YAHUITLALPAN,
ZAUTLA, PUEBLA

Ulises Márquez Nava

Kind of programme and educational level

A bilingual curriculum project based on the local culture. The aim is to cover educational needs in a population that is lagging behind educationally, and to improve living conditions in the community as a whole.

Geographical and administrative aspects

San Andres Yahuitlalpan is located in the Sierra Norte of the state of Puebla, in the southern central region of Mexico.

The school covers boys and girls from the community, although students from other communities nearby that lack educational services also attend. This initiative was generated by an NGO and taken under the responsibility of the corresponding School Supervisory Department.

Indigenous target group(s)

Nahuatl, in the Nahuat linguistic variant, corresponding to the area of Nahuatl-Totonaca contact in the east of Mexico

Programme description

The *telesecundarias* (tele-secondary schools) constitute a subsystem of secondary schools (basic middle-school education) from Grades 7 to 9 whereby a single teacher works with each grade, together with the support of televised transmissions on all the curriculum topics. It has resulted in an excellent system for extending educational services, though the results reached in terms of learning achievement are heterogeneous – which is a subject beyond the scope of this analysis.

In the present case, we are identifying the school as a 'tele-school', although – while it belongs to that administrative system – the educational programme does not follow the corresponding format. It does, however, use video recordings for supporting teaching on various elements of the national curriculum.

This area of the Sierra Norte of the state of Puebla has a sub-humid, temperate climate, with occasional summer rains and ecosystems with high, wooded areas. The community lies in a mountainous terrain with an altitude varying between 1,900 and 2,950 metres above sea level. Yahutlapan – one of thirty-one communities which make up the municipality of Zautla – is one of the poorest and most marginalized communities in the country.

Background: legal-political, socio-economic, educational and linguistic situation

The major source of income is temporary migration for unqualified labourers to cities and agricultural areas close by. In recent years, illegal temporary migrations to the US of young people, both male and female, has increased considerably with all its attendant problems.

As of the 1920s, Mexico has carried out educational actions focused on indigenous peoples, and since 1978 this has constituted a subsystem within the Ministry of Education (SEP[1]). This has served as a model for other countries, particularly in Latin America. Nevertheless, even today only initial education (up to 4 years of age), pre-school and primary (up to Grade 6) is covered by the system, and for the year 2000 only 43.4 per cent of existing educational demand was covered.[2]

In addition, the official focus of indigenous education up to quite recently had as its objective successively to 'integrate the indigenous people to the Mexican nationality', 'to break with the backwardness of centuries and to reach the ... modernization of indigenous Mexico', 'a policy of assimilation of the indigenous peoples to the dominant forms of the Nation', to 'promote cultural change' and the teaching of Spanish. In fact up until the present, two ideological tendencies around indigenous questions are still evident, but neither questions the objective of integration: The *indigenismo* (thinking on indigenous issues) of the right and that of the left. The first proposes integration as a nationalist imperative ... the second as a nationalist and as a class imperative. [3]

Nowadays the discourse has more to do with the strengthening of cultural diversity and the construction of interculturality. However this has not modified the conceptions and even less the practice of the teachers. The indigenous school is still seen as a means of integration and for teaching Spanish.

In addition, the opinion of indigenous peoples has not been sought with regard to their need for the school nor the role this should play. It is true that the perception of its importance is now clearly established, even though to a large extent it is considered (in an ambivalent kind of way) [4] as a factor for social mobility.

In general, if the rural areas have the largest concentration of poverty in Mexico, the poorest and most marginalized are those where the indigenous groups are located. This generates seasonal migratory movements to improve subsistence levels, which take the form of a to-ing and fro-ing between the city and the countryside. This has an enormous influence on conceptions of the good life, of social relations and the need for schooling (and the loss of the mother tongue, or at least the appropriation of the national language, Spanish) with the attendant consequences.

In these conditions, material poverty is reinforced by a 'poor school', as much in its material conditions of operation and management, as in the results which it obtains. This has been shown by studies in which the indigenous school is at the lowest levels in terms of efficiency, quality and relevance.[5]

With this combination of factors, indigenous peoples are facing an unprecedented process of cultural erosion. They are pressured inordinately by an excluding, consumer-based society that – by means of different messages (including those spread by electronic media) – puts their survival as indigenous people at high risk.

Furthermore, in the case of Mexico there is no specific provision for secondary education for indigenous populations (nor is there any planned). Very few therefore have access to this level, and those who do, study at schools which do not correspond to their characteristics, needs and expectations.

The institution has since its creation in 1989 offered an appropriate quality education conceived as a factor in the development of the community and the region. The school is based on and sustained by the fundamental purpose of generating an educational resource that makes a contribution to the reconstruction of human dignity of the individuals and the social group involved. The concern is to redefine the current group identity, in such a way as to make the social group more autonomous in its own identity and better equipped to deal with other groups in society.

Objectives and focus

A fundamental challenge is to 'place culture at the centre of the educational act', not only through the inclusion of local content but also with a view to looking at the educational process altogether and in response to the characteristics of the community. The community principles are used as the basis of the learning process, and the mother tongue is fundamental for the construction of this knowledge. Another important aspect is the question of the utility of the school, which, to compensate for educational lag, should generate a means of transforming the community (through actions to improve production, environmental conservation, and improvement in the quality of life) and allow for the continued learning of students after school.

Participation

Originally the idea for the school came from a reflection on the participation of indigenous students of the community in the general tele-secondary school that was located in Yahuitlalpan: for three consecutive terms, with an average annual enrolment of twenty-five students, only two indigenous students had entered per year, and none had finished First Grade. Thus, the team in charge of the school set itself up to develop a programme that would answer the needs of the indigenous community in which it was situated. The initial proposal therefore comes from social actions outside the community concerned as much with regional development as with indigenous issues.

In the application for the proposal, the participation of university-level indigenous students has been significant[6]. They work on the identification, selection, and pedagogical adjustment of local content, as well as in the articulation of this local content with the national curriculum. This process also implies collaboration with the elders of the community. Parents too need to be convinced of the new model, so that they will let their children come to school.

The relationship with the community was deliberately planned, as explained in the didactic strategies outlined in the next section. In this way, different members of the community became involved in the process – sometimes as 'informants' for the teachers' team,[7] and sometimes as informants/counsellors and trainers of the students themselves, and as evaluators of the work carried out and of learning achievement.

On the other hand the implementation and sustainability of the experience was directly related to the support given by the School Supervisory Department for the tele-secondary schools. The interest shown by the Supervisor for a proposal appropriate for local conditions, and his intercession with parents to vouch for the validity of the studies in the school, were crucial.

The core principle is the implementation of a teaching method which relies on community life and makes it the centre of learning. In this respect, six specific strategies which lead to learning processes were developed:

Methods used

1. Appropriation of language as a core for the expression of identity. Through the recuperation[8] of their own word or language (in this case Nahuatl), and through the mastery of the common language (i.e. Spanish, the national language and lingua franca for communicating with other peoples), the purpose is to develop in the students the ability to express several facets of their identity. By developing the capacity to talk about their own re-valued and re-signified words, and by furthering their knowledge of the national language, the students strengthen their own identity and develop as future citizens.

2. Education as a means of recuperating and giving new value to identity uses the educational processes and spaces to give central importance to identity-building through the socio-cultural praxis of the group. The idea is to conceive of education as a means of recuperating and revaluing elements which express cultural identity, not just through mechanical repetition but also, and above all, through introduction to systems of interpretation of the world, of their relation to the world and their relation to 'others'.

3. Incorporating the everyday experience of the educational process into the sociocultural praxis of the group and the community through a school that is open to, focused on, and participating in community life (fiestas, ceremonies, group activities [faenas], social and political acts). An education process that is capable of recognizing,

and incorporating, the relationship between people and their environment, and which itself generates knowledge and shares it with the community, in this way contributing to the improvement of the living conditions in the society in question.

4. Incorporating the networks of popular knowledge into the educational process, in particular with those people who share their knowledge amongst themselves: mothers and grandmothers who teach the children how to work with wool and to embroider; other specialists who teach young people the names and uses of different plants; and fathers who teach their sons how to work with clay, palm leaves or stone.

5. Technical knowledge: the promotion through education of an understanding of one's relation with the environment, by examining what crops and plants are cultivated and the possible cultural reasons for this, while also considering techniques and procedures that are both viable and useful and that can improve quality of life

6. Establishing an educational community. Reproducing in the school the ancestral values of the group: community life, solidarity, joint responsibility and commitment, through forms of organization and conviviality that allow the construction of new forms of relations on an equal basis, both between men and women and between generations.

Curriculum/Themes

With a view to overcoming teachers' strong traditional association of study programmes with schoolwork, it was decided that the curriculum should be organized around five workshops[9] so that from the start the concept of knowledge being related to a particular subject was modified. In this way, we were looking to orient our work towards the collective construction of learning by breaking the mould of the traditional teacher-pupil relationship.

Each of the workshops includes contents from the national curriculum linked with local contents, so as to ensure that all learning is related to local issues. The workshops are the following:

1. *Workshop on Community Activities*
   Focused on organizational, social, and cultural activities, and on rituals having to do with the productive and reproductive cycles of the families and the community as a whole. The recording, analysis and appreciation of these activities is carried out in conjunction with elements of the curriculum on Social Sciences. Local history, memory and oral tradition is also considered and contrasted with documents from various sources. There is a special emphasis on the collective project as a community project and students' views of what constitutes a good life. The aim is to reconcile future possibilities with achievable goals.

2. *Science Workshop*
   This covers the systematic study of local knowledge with regard to certain themes and contrasts, or complements this with elements of Western science. The aim is to bring these two knowledge systems closer together. Themes include: health, nutrition, taxonomy or 'organization of the world', geography, physics and chemistry. The study of the body in its physical and biological dimension is important and this is framed within a life project approach of each individual in the community and based on ethnic identity.

3. *Workshop on Expression*
   This occupies a central place in the process of training of the students. It covers the mastery of the languages of the school (their own language and the common language) as much from the point of view of its technical aspects (grammar, orthography and syntax) as well as its communicative function in society.

Part of the workshop is concerned with drafting and systematizing knowledge coming out of other workshops so that these are discussed and appropriated. The oral tradition and the creation of individual texts is also part of the workshop activities. The workshop has fixed amounts of time for both Nahuatl and Spanish in the timetable.

4.   ***Numbers Workshop***

In this workshop the focus is on the expression of reality in symbolic languages (mathematics, graphics), as well as on the utilization of mathematics as a tool for the understanding of diverse phenomena and for the solution of problems. Mathematics and physics are taught at students' grade level in this workshop. It is important to point out that this workshop focuses on the systematic construction of tools of formal thought that support the cognitive development of the students.

5.   ***Production Workshop***

The aim of this workshop is to develop students' technical capacity to improve their own family's and the community's living conditions. This is organized by semesters in which students participate in horticultural production, fruit growing, baking, carpentry, recycling of waste paper, and rearing of small farm animals. In this way they learn some job skills and help diversify their family's food production.

The work focuses on fusing the competencies and knowledge the students bring to the classroom with what they learn in formal education. It is based firmly on the networks of traditional knowledge for the building and strengthening of cultural identity.

Altogether nine 'cultural fields' are dealt with in the workshops, and these are considered as being fundamental to the integration of a thematic universe of indigenous communities:

1. Content with regard to local knowledge articulated with the normative contents of the respective grade level in the areas of Science and Technology

2. Knowledge and values placed within memory and historical time, both of the community and the group, so that the local becomes contextualized in the framework of historical national processes, while at the same time these processes are placed in a local perspective

3. The recognition of community and group spaces, which implies, on the one hand, *physical space* – in geographical terms and in regard to the ecosystem – and its articulation with the normative contents of the corresponding academic curricula, and, on the other hand, the recognition of *collective spaces,* and their articulation to the normative contents of Social Sciences.

Three cultural fields refer to identity:

4. Reflection on personal identity, to allow for the possibility of building a personal vision, thereby developing individual learning projects and competencies

5. Giving new meaning to cultural and ethnic identity on the basis of the local culture and the search for a full and dignified life

6. Knowledge and values that give national identity (history, geography and civic education) in such a way as to contribute to the strengthening of intercultural relations.

Two fields refer to language:

7. That which has to do with the local language, Nahuatl, in regard to the oral tradition, the production of texts, as a means of communication and as a language with a structure

8.   In regard to the common language of all Mexicans, Spanish, in order to speak to others and express what one is and what one wants to be.

And finally, a field which refers to the structures of thought and the use of mathematics:

9.   The field of contents which encourage the development of the capacity for formal reasoning and symbolic expression.

Language(s) of instruction

The school emphasizes the use of Nahuatl as a language of instruction as well as a language of communication. Most of the activities, discussions and dialogues are conducted in this language. In the workshop on expression in Nahuatl, the language is also covered as an object of study, and students are taught to understand it better.

Nevertheless, most of the learning materials are in Spanish, and a mastery of the Spanish language will be necessary for those students who wish to continue their studies or even be involved in society outside the community. For these reasons, Spanish is also used in the school, especially for reference materials, and it is also a subject of academic study so that students can improve their knowledge of it. In this way, both languages play an important role in the educational process and the school. Undoubtedly, though, Nahuatl is used more.

Teachers/Training

With one exception, [10] those responsible for teaching in the school are graduates of the degree course in Development Planning of the Centre for Studies for Rural Development (CESDER), with a specialization in Rural Education. [11] This training, however, does not have the specificity of bilingual education as part of the curriculum, so it was necessary to establish initial training programmes (beginning from the moment one joins the staff) and an accompanying support programme.

Teachers join the school only at the beginning of the school year. As a preparatory activity, they participate in a training workshop where they learn to use the teaching method through 'working cards' [12] and the way in which contents are articulated in the nine cultural fields.

Throughout the year teachers in the school work as a collegial team to articulate and enrich the activities of the three grades. In this way, feedback between each group on its activities, as well as the monitoring of students' progress, helps advance the process. Both processes are supported by advisors from CESDER and the school zone who work to resolve problems and improve the team. This support varies in its frequency and depends on who is in the team, since the more experienced teachers require less support.

Materials and activities

At secondary level there are practically no materials available in indigenous languages. Fortunately in the case of Nahuatl some bilingual dictionaries are available, as well as grammars and works of literature (classical from the colonial period, as well as recent literature), especially poetry as well as some transcriptions of the oral tradition. A related problem is that they are in various dialects of Nahuatl; however this can be turned to advantage as it allows for comparative revisions between the different forms of the language.

There are no textbooks except for the first grades of primary school (generally with a slant towards teaching Spanish), and there are also some rough manuals prepared by recent literates. Thus, one task that the school has taken on from the very beginning has been the production of its own learning materials as a result of its workshop activities. For the most part these are small booklets of 'domestic' production that permit us to preserve and reproduce local knowledge as well as the relation with 'school' knowledge.

The school has its own library – resource centre, with materials in both Nahuatl and Spanish, as well as videos, and material dealing with production processes both from an intercultural as well as a manufacturing point of view. Currently we are experimenting with some of the teachers in producing electronic materials for bilingual learning as much for our students as for younger children and adults.

Outcomes

A first result among both students and the community as a whole has been a transformation in the value given to the local language and culture. The language is now used more publicly, while the culture is disseminated in a more permanent way.

As for the students, they have become young people with a strengthened sense of cultural identity, secure in their actions, and with pride in their own origins as a foundation. In addition, the levels of school achievement in the high school and the university are such that there are no differences between the indigenous and non-indigenous students at the same level. There are now more than a dozen of these young people following various courses of study at university with no greater difficulty than their peers.

In addition to the improvement in the quality of educational services and the enhanced validity in the National Education System (especially through Further Education), there has been a greater involvement of parents in the school, as previously mentioned, as informants and advisers and evaluators of the process.

This project has been visited by representatives of different indigenous groups in Mexico who have heard of its existence. [13] Inspired by the work they observed they have created secondary schools in their own regions, with their own proposals. In this regard we have shared our methodology for working with traditional authorities, local teachers, and, in the case of Wixarika, with universities.

With the creation of the National Co-ordination for Intercultural Education, within the structure of the SEP, the educational proposal has been reviewed with a view to orienting quality education services in other regions of the country and even proposing it as open to international review.

It is only when people take ownership of these kinds of proposals that their institutionalization becomes possible. This ownership has to include their involvement in the definition of contents and ways of dealing with them, as well as in the follow up and evaluation of the work of the institution in co-ordination with the educational authorities.

Lessons learnt: values and objects

The role that teachers have in the process is crucial. The ideal situation is one where the teachers come from the indigenous culture in which the project itself is developed, as long as they also have a solid professional training, which should also be adapted to circumstances (ad hoc) and of a high quality.

The educational authorities play a fundamental role in the consolidation of these processes. The acceptance of proposals of this kind – which demonstrate not only the capacity to respond with speed and efficiency to needs, but also to incorporate local content into an educational process that is in dialogue with national curricula – should occur at the administrative levels (in this case, the school supervisor), as well as at the higher echelons. If not, these will remain just isolated experiences, with little impact on broader educational policy for indigenous peoples. [14]

The relationship between the school and the community should be as organic as possible, so that knowledge flows between the two, making the school space not just a context for the socialization and learning of the boys and girls, but above all a space that injects energy into the life of the community and supports the construction of viable community projects.

This, of course, demands that the *school* community maintain the sense of belonging to the *local* community. It means that no separation should be established such as that which is common in most educational establishments in relation to the societies to which they belong.

These experiences need to be made 'visible' to the local and regional population's decision-makers, policy-makers and planners in order to guarantee their sustainability over time irrespective of shifts in public educational policy. Obviously, this demands a constant revision of content so that it responds to the changing dynamics of the community and to innovations and changes in education in general.

With a view to the future building of equitable and harmonious intercultural relations and the construction of curricula for intercultural education in national education systems, it is absolutely indispensable to consider providing quality education for indigenous peoples at other levels of the education system.

Duration   1989 to 2001

Finance and budget   Since 1993 the school has been a Work Centre that is part of the public school system in the Mexican education sector. The teachers' salaries, investment in the school infrastructure and some maintenance costs are paid for out of public funds.

The community provides materials as well as the work force for the day-to-day maintenance of the school.

The CESDER (Centre for Studies for Rural Development), the NGO behind the project, provided a budget between 1989 and 1993 for its total support. From then until 2001 funds were transferred for the school cafeteria[15] as well as for the acquisition of learning materials and for the hiring of some young teachers during certain periods. The amounts would be difficult to quantify since they are irregularly distributed.

Institution responsible   School Supervisory Department 016 – Tepexoxuca de Telesecundarias Estatales (School Supervision 016 – Tepexoxuca of State Tele-Secondary Schools)
Cesder-Prodes, A.C.

Ulises Márquez Nava   Contact
Asesor del proyecto
CESDER-PRODES, A.C.
AP. 47, Tlatlauquitepec, Pue.,
73900 MÉXICO (dirección postal)
Capolihtic s/n,
Zautla, Pue.,
MEXICO
Tel: [+52] (55) 5329 0995, ext. 7501
Fax: [+52] (233) 318 0321
E-mail: ulises_cesder@hotmail.com
educacion@cesder-prodes.org.mx
Website: http://www.cesder-prodes.org.mx

NOTES

1. Initially as 'Mexican Rural School' (1922), 'Houses of the People' (1923), 'Cultural Missions' (1925), 'Department of Indian Incorporation' (1926), 'Department of Cultural Missions' (1927), 'Centres of Indigenous Education' (1933), 'Institute of Literacy in Indigenous Languages' (1945), 'Direction on Indigenous Affairs/Issues/SEP' (1946), and 'General Direction of Indigenous Education/SEP' (1978).
2. Cf: Webpage of the General Direction of Indigenous Education, SEP, México: http://www.sep.gob.mx/wb2/sep/sep_4413_informacion_basica_g
3. References from 'Información sobre la Dirección General de Educación Indígena: Antecedentes'. Cf: http://www.sep.gob.mx/wb2/sep/sep_4409_antecedentes.
4. On the one hand, they complain about the loss of what is their own, most of all of the values of those generations that have not gone to school, but on the other they recognize that school helps them to be less discriminated against and affords social mobility.
5. One study includes the geographical area of influence of the school. Cf: Schmelkes, Sylvia (1993): 'La calidad de la educación primaria en México. Estudio de cinco regiones en el estado de Puebla'. México: CEE

6. The degree in Rural Development Planning offered by CESDER.

7. For the identification, understanding and localization of cultural elements.

8. In terms of understanding the language and its structures as well as its use in communications.

9. Originally four: The Science Workshop was added to the curriculum after the first term as a specific space for science content.

10. Initially trained as a teacher at secondary level and specialized in Teaching Social Sciences designated by the Secretary of Public Education of the State.

11. Although the national requirement is that teachers should have degrees in education, the graduates from CESDER are recognized for their professional capacities. The bulk of teachers in the School Area 016–Tepexoxuca, on which this school depends, are graduated from this degree course therefore.

12. A planning system which starts off with cultural contents and places them in relation with national curriculum indicating activities, expected results, special criteria and evaluation mechanisms. Of variable duration between one to six weeks they allow the organization of the work in the workshop in an integrated way.

13. Wixarika (pronunce 'virrarika'), known as the 'Huicholes', of the State of Jalisco; Raramuri, known as the 'Tarahumaras', of the State of Chihuahua; and Tseltales, of the State of Chiapas.

14. In the case in question, the need to mobilize teachers within the school area and the difficulty of their insertion into other less specific models led the School Supervisor to decide on substantial modifications to the curriculum and the operation of the school in 2001. In this way the model was not continued even though it maintains some aspects complementary to the educational proposal 'tele-secondary linked to the community'. In almost all schools of the School Area 016–Tepexoxuca of tele-secondary schools.

15. Which offered meals to students to improve nutritional levels. Since 1998 the service was reduced by request of the parents, so that the children come home earlier.

MEXICO:
TRAINING OF INDIGENOUS FARMERS TO RUN COMMUNITY FORESTRY ENTERPRISES

Rodolfo López Arzola

Non-formal education: Community technical education

Type of programme and educational level

This project covers the whole of the state of Oaxaca with its 2,000 communities, including 200 possessing woods and forests of commercial value and owning or holding 85 per cent of all the forest in the state.

Geographical and administrative scope

Indigenous communities: Zapotecs, Chatinos, Zoques, etc.

Indigenous target group(s)

The project is set in a context of considerable marginalization due to the poverty, migration and illiteracy prevalent in the rural areas of southern Mexico. The programme involves building a popular economy by bolstering an entrepreneurial and social culture as an alternative to poverty, thereby giving pride of place both to community participation and to the promotion and shaping of a social entrepreneurial culture. It seeks to enable farmers to run an enterprise in all its technical aspects on their own and with the education they have, typically four to six years of primary schooling.

  This process was carried out by constructing and appropriating a self-management development model

Description of programme

Summary

meeting the needs of the Zapotec, Chatino, Zoque and other indigenous communities on the basis of sustainable use of their natural resources and through their cultural structures.

The project focused on training adults to act as managers and technicians in their enterprises. At the same time, the students were given training to improve their skills for community living.

*   From 1982 to 2000: 1,000 adults (entrepreneurial and technical activities)
*   From 1990 to 2000: 1,680 students (community skills)
*   From 1990 to 2000: 600 women (micro-management).

Background: legal-political, socio-economic, educational and linguistic situation

The state of Oaxaca covers an area of 95,000 km^2 and is split into eight geographical regions inhabited by 21 ethnic groups. It comprises 30 districts taking in 570 municipalities, of which 280 (49.12 per cent) are rural; these in turn are subdivided into 7,210 localities. There is a wide variety of climates and ecological systems within the one state, which is characterized by a mountainous terrain and marked contrasts.

Marginalization in Mexico is mainly to be found in the centre and south of the country, being very high in the states of Oaxaca, Chiapas and Guerrero, which together make up the southern Pacific region. Oaxaca is considered one of the country's poorest states, with high poverty, migration and illiteracy rates. There are practically no development zones in the countryside.

The state has a total population of 3,019,560, of whom 48.9 per cent are men and 51.1 per cent women, with a predominance of children and young people. Of the total population, 42.6 per cent are under the age of 15, and only 4.7 per cent are over 65 years. Furthermore, the population is fundamentally indigenous and organized in communities where the uses and practices of traditional socialization and formation are prevalent.

The economically active male and female population is 39.24 per cent, of which some 68.28 per cent corresponds to men and 12.33 per cent to women. Of all females under five years of age, 39.1 per cent speak some indigenous language and 23.9 per cent of females speaking an indigenous language are monolingual, that is, do not speak Spanish.

With regard to education, 67 per cent of the total population of the state are behind, in that they lack basic education (INEGI, 2000). The female population aged between 6 and 14 years able to read and write represents 82.1 per cent. Illiteracy increases in women over 40, reaching 60.6 per cent. Female illiteracy stands at 34.6 per cent, since 312,014 women aged 15 and over are registered as unable to read and write (INEGI, 1995).

PROJECT BACKGROUND

Exploitation of the pine forests by Fábricas de Papel (FAPATUX), a semi-public company, and by the private company Compañía Forestal de Oaxaca (CFO) – which together for twenty-five years had a concession in Sierra Norte and Sierra Sur – saw the profits whisked off elsewhere in exchange for rock-bottom remuneration of the community, while the resource itself deteriorated rapidly.

FAPATUX, with federal support, had received a 25-year concession (1957-81) to work the pine forests of the communities of the Sierra Juarez and the state. The communities received material benefits and employment, though only as labourers and not in specialist areas. However, selective felling of the best timber, the lack of soil and water conservation, and the failure to replant all prompted protests from the communities.

FAPATUX tried in 1981 to secure a new concession to continue working the forests, but the communities opposed this flatly, which refusal gave rise at state and national level to the Organization for Defence of the Natural Resources of the Sierra Juarez (ODRENASIJ), formed by community members and local and outside professionals. The organization won the fight against forestry mismanagement and the bad forestry policy that had been a far cry from anything to do with development. Apart from being spontaneous, however, the organization was ephemeral since it disappeared as such upon accomplishing that task, chiefly because it had no alternative to offer the communities.

As part of this movement, the communities won legal protection that left their forests free as of 1982. With the recovery of their forests, the originally campesino communities discovered that their interpretation of the benefits of the forest was more cultural than anything else; they had yet to learn the culture of utilizing the timber. At that time a federal government team, under a programme called Forest Development, began promoting and organizing community forestry enterprises as an alternative – hence the need to train one's own human resources with respect to forestry resources, in terms both of technicians and of community members.

They thus set up Community Forestry Enterprises (EFCs) managed by the community members themselves and adapted to their usage and customs, structures, appointment mechanisms and rotation systems.

The Forest Development team then set itself up as ASTECO, A.C. The ASTECO team formed twenty-five community forestry enterprises, the first union of forest communities and the first organization in the state for defence of their rights in dealings with the Ministry of Finance and Public Credit.

There are at present, on an annual basis, more than seventy community forestry enterprises operating in the state of Oaxaca.

Objectives and focus The primary objective is to enable the campesinos to run the administrative, financial, accounting and marketing aspects of an enterprise on their own and with the education they have (typically four to six years of primary schooling).

The indigenous communities have centuries of experi- **Participation**
ence in the matter of electing leaders in a general assembly. They follow the same process when it comes to picking people to manage the forestry enterprises and for all decisions having to do with community living.

Training follows the method known as 'transfer-appro- **Methods used**
priation', which means delegating knowledge and skills so that they can be mastered and applied. It also incorporates the model of communal auditing for the biannual review of bookkeeping, where capacity-building is entrusted to young people, who in turn train as future EFC managers.

Capacity-building and training are in accordance with the community structure and mechanisms, usage and customs. It is customary in these communities for men, from the age of 18, to take on a series of posts or duties in the form of free service to the community. This may involve anything from being a messenger to such duties as presiding over the municipality in the civil structure and also in the communal-agrarian structure or the Church. This lasts until the age of 60. They are allowed some years off in the intervening period and then once more appointed step by step to other duties. They thereby acquire a great deal of skill and knowledge before occupying a post in the enterprises.

Spanish. Spanish is used since in many communities the **Language of instruction**
original language is no longer spoken.

Training is provided in the following areas: **Curriculum/Themes**

- administration, accounting, auditing
- fiscal norms and laws
- forest management – nurseries, reforestation, pests

- sawmilling, road design, and
- computing.

Teachers/Training

The project started with a team of government professionals seeking to transfer their academic knowledge to the indigenous learners. The professionals provided training in the practice of supervising the processes of appropriation of administrative sciences by the indigenous people concerned. Rather than courses, it was an initial stage.

An intensive introduction was given for each subject and the students were subsequently supervised in their respective tasks. Account was taken here of the experience acquired by the indigenous appointees in their education and training systems (through community service) that initiate them from the age of 18; and we 'grafted' the academic knowledge by means of bridging systems.

Materials and activities

Students used textbooks designed by professionals that provided introductory mathematics courses of the most elementary kind. Calculators were also used, by all managers. The level of complexity was then raised until students were initiated to their specialization. For example, those whose speciality was accountancy would work their way up to analysis of financial statements, sales control, and so on. Under the same procedure, but with more time, they were subsequently introduced to using computer systems.

The people whom we worked with possessed little formal education but had been appointed in the general assembly of their respective communities. Every two or three years these assemblies changed all their officers, with the result that we were constantly training different people.

Outcomes

The transfer-appropriation method was conducive to the capacity-building and training of managerial staff for the community forestry enterprises (EFCs). In thirteen years, knowledge of the various areas covered was transferred to 653 community members, 156 women and 865 primary school children.

In 1983 the Forest Development team had formed twelve EFCs and a more definite capacity-building and training programme in the following areas: administration, accounting, auditing, fiscal norms and laws, forest management (nurseries, reforestation, pests), sawmilling industry, road design, and computing. Thirteen years later, there were eighty-one EFCs (1995).

Lessons learnt: strengths and weaknesses

Most current models of development seek to create permanent employment and generate wealth as basic objectives among others, on the theory that only with the maximum number of university-trained professionals is it possible to attain these goals, since it is they who have to manage the enterprises and institutions, and hence all the requisite processes, particularly where economics is concerned.

Yet this assumption was stood on its head in the case of some community forestry enterprises in Oaxaca, which in the 1982 – 95 period proved that other sequences could be incorporated to meet the goals of employment and wealth generation, without any professional component in the operation.

While this also implies a big investment in specialized consultancy, the outlay is much smaller when compared with the investment of the formal academic structure, and smaller still when set against the high social cost for a community of having its own (professional) elements but with an ideological deformation at odds or incompatible with community interests.

For indigenous rural development in Mexico, what is needed is to design flexible systems that are suited to specific situations, rather than trying to adapt these situations to systems dreamed up in some office. One of the lessons is that some accompaniment is needed in the day-to-day activities of the enterprises concerned, where ad hoc systems, that can be 'grafted' onto their community structures, are called for.

Another lesson is that the attention must be individualized, community by community and enterprise by enterprise, rather than provided en masse and with serial courses.

It was likewise seen that without a willingness on both sides to transfer and to appropriate the knowledge, it was hard to devise the best instructional methods.

Weak points

The fact that the communities change their leaders every two to three years, and that the latter do not make use of their experience, represents a cost for the community, as well as delaying the operation of the enterprises for six months. The outgoing trained managers do not transfer their knowledge to the incoming people over and above the bare operational minimum required.

The cost of this accompaniment is high and the enterprises must be willing to pay for it. In addition, the fact that the system runs without professionally trained management hampers its ability to make those adaptive changes (either external or internal) that are dictated by the market, a limitation that has implications for the economic survival of the enterprises.

Duration

In 1982, the Forest Development team organized a first pilot experiment in the Zapotec community of Santa Catarina Ixtepeji, in the Sierra de Juarez range, where a first community forestry enterprise was established to inaugurate the project, which continued until 2002. In that period the indigenous entrepreneurial culture regarding forestry was consolidated to the point of serving as an example nationally and internationally. The World Bank even held it up as a model in a special programme that it is now planned to reproduce in other Mexican states with a great deal of capacity-building support in various productive aspects of the indigenous communities, but in keeping with a more paternalistic mindset.

The project was initially supported by the Federal Government and subsequently by the enterprises themselves, which paid us for the training and consultancy. Recently the World Bank and the Federal Government have been meeting these costs.

Financing/Budget

Asesoría Técnica a Comunidades Oaxaqueñas (technical consultancy for Oaxaca communities)

Responsible organization/institution

Rodolfo López Arzola
Presidente de la Asesoría Técnica a Comunidades Oaxaqueñas (ASETECO)
Eucaliptos No. 320
Col. Reforma C.P. 68050
Mexico City
Mexico
Tel./Fax 951 5131730
Tel. 951 51 34424
Email: Asetecooax@infosel.net.mx
Roloar@spersaoaxaca.com.mx

Contact

Notes, References and Information Available:

The evaluation was finalized in 2003 with the publication of the book *Una caminata de 20 años en los bosques comunales de Oaxaca* (A 20-year journey in the communal forests of Oaxaca). The purpose of this ASETECO book was to have the voices of the various actors in the forestry sector heard and to relate a more complete and impartial story, unlike the various versions so far brought out by the Government and some NGOs.

López Arzola, R.; Jesús Góngora, M. 'Experiencia de 13 años (1982 – 1995) en la formación de directivos campesinos indígenas en y para actividades empresariales en el Estado de Oaxaca' (Thirteen years' experience (1982–95) in the training of indigenous campesino managers in and for entrepreneurial activities in the state of Oaxaca), paper submitted at the National Forum on challenges and prospects of adult education in Mexico, 13 – 15 November 1994, Mexico City. Convened by UPN, INEA, CREFAL, CEAAL and SEP.

Ramírez Domínguez, R. 'El manejo comunitario de los recursos forestales: una opción para las comunidades campesinas' (The community management of forest resources: an option for the campesino communities), paper submitted at the Seminar on challenges and America, 23 – 26 November 1998, Oaxaca, Oaxaca. Convened by Methodus, PSSM, GAIA, UPISL and SEM-ARNAP, Oaxaca.

NEW ZEALAND:
TE REO PUTAIAO SCIENCE PROJECT

Janet Nairn

Science Programme at Rotorua Boys' High School (RBHS), Bilingual Department. Four-year trial, from 1999 to 2002

Type of programme and educational level

Secondary School, Rotorua, New Zealand

Geographical and administrative level

Rotorua Boys' High bilingual-unit students, focusing on motivating under-achieving Maori students. Fifty-four at-risk students have participated over four years.

Indigenous target group(s)

The lack of involvement and achievement of Maori students in science has long been an area of concern for schools. In 2000, the 'Innovations Funding Pool for Students at Risk' provided funding to trial a programme that aimed to increase the motivation, confidence, and scientific learning of selected *Te Reo* students from the RBHS Bilingual Department. The programme aimed to develop and apply innovative teaching methods to 'at-risk' and under-achieving Maori students. Success of the programme would be quantified by improved academic results and social behaviour.

Description of programme

Summary

The programme has achieved many of its objectives. It has been well received by the boys, their *whanau* (extended family), and their peers. Students have developed good routines for working on science activities, the relevance of science is motivating achievement, and mentor support has become an effective focusing tool.

In addition to these achievements, the programme has also provided challenges in staffing, timetabling, and resourcing. The retention of many of the boys into senior science meant the programme was financing more boys and activities than planned, and the introduction of the *hauora* (health and well-being) model into Grades 9 and 10 mainstream classes increased the workload. The time allocation for recording all the evaluation data requested was grossly underestimated.

Background

Rotorua Boys' High School is the oldest secondary school in Rotorua, New Zealand, and is committed to providing an excellent education for young men. The school enjoys national recognition for its academic excellence, for its sporting achievements and for the quality of its cultural endeavours. The school offers a wide range of national curriculum and local subjects. One half (50 per cent) of the 1,198 students are Maori. Many of the targeted at-risk boys come from struggling socio-economic backgrounds.

The original idea for setting up a programme at Rotorua Boys' High School (RBHS) to motivate Maori students to achieve in science came from a *Ngati Whakuae kaumatua* (respected local figure or leader), Bishop Kingi. His concern at the lack of local Maori able to make informed decisions on science-related *Iwi* (people) issues prompted him to encourage greater participation of Maori students in RBHS science classes. The 'Innovations Funding Pool for Students at Risk' provided funding to trial a programme that aimed to increase the motivation, confidence, and scientific learning of students from the RBHS Bilingual Department. This trial *Te Reo Putaiao* programme was initially aimed at Maori students, whose lack of involvement and achievement in science has long been an area of concern for schools.

The programme aimed to catch the imagination of 'at-risk' and under-achieving students by developing and applying innovative teaching methods to a group of selected *Te Reo* students. Success of the programme would be quantified by improved academic results and social behaviour of the students. The programme would provide them with increased motivation to learn, and confidence to undertake projects, and to accept leadership responsibilities. Increased self-esteem would follow their becoming knowledgeable and informed members of their *Iwi*. Familiarity with some of the skills needed to cope with modern society would increase employment opportunities. Educational qualifications were to be targeted through Unit Standards in science, computing and forestry. Computer confidence and literacy would be further increased, with skills applied in community projects.

The long-term aim was to further develop the methods and technologies so they could be applied across the whole spectrum of at-risk students.

Objectives and focus

Even though parents and elders did not participate in the design of the curriculum and the selection of delivery methods, parents in particular were invited to view and review the programme, to ask questions or to make suggestions as they saw fit. Parents received regular newsletters about the programme and regularly visited the school whare (a Maori hut or house). The newsletters provided information on student progress, fund-raising for off-site trips and details of proposed activities. At the start of the trial, some of the mothers cooked breakfasts after the boys finished their fitness swim programmes. One method used to encourage parents to participate was a 'mothers and sons' lesson. The sons became the teachers and supported their mothers through the activity.

Maori speakers and visitors were invited to the programme and the boys enjoyed listening to the experiences of others, especially Maori with high

Participation

achievements in sports. Parents, the students themselves, their mentors and providers were provided with
several opportunities to participate in the ongoing evaluation of the programme and to evaluate the programme
delivery.

Methods used   At-risk students encounter many barriers to learning,
including: irregular attendance, lack of confidence in
writing and numeracy skills, lack of interest in science,
irrelevant learning contexts, unsuitable teaching strategies, and poor self-esteem resulting from previous
school failures. Mentor-driven *hauora* (health and well-
being) activities were established to remove many of the
barriers that confronted these students, by providing
(when necessary): uniforms, resources, food, mentor
support and transport. They also boosted students' self-
esteem and much-valued social image through fitness
training, off-site science trips, participation in courses
(social skills, parenting and personal health), and motivational speakers. Further, to overcome these barriers,
the programme used two methodologies:

1.   *Innovative teaching methods* were selected for their
     originality, student appeal and unthreatening
     nature. They had to be activity-based and rele-
     vant, and included intensive use of computer
     technology, along with off-site trips and relevant
     learning contexts. These methods have made sci-
     ence considerably more interesting and relevant
     to at-risk students.
2.   *Motivational strategies* were selected to overcome
     poor attendance and lack of interest, self-disci-
     pline and confidence. These strategies included
     the appointment of external mentors from
     Fletcher Challenge Forests (FCF) staff (2000) and
     then an RBHS mentor (2001), who was appointed
     as an RBHS staff member. An extended early-
     morning school timetable was followed by
     breakfast.

Eight strategies for improvement:

1. Using a science/technology context and a variety of local science-based industries to change the behaviour of at-risk boys in the school's bilingual unit

2. Developing a support network with a large local industry – Fletcher Challenge Forests – involving mentoring and workplace visits

3. Using Maori-speaking mentors from Fletcher Challenge Forests to support the students in their learning and achievement

4. Introducing intense, high-impact, off-site, out-of-comfort-zone learning experiences at the end of each term as motivation and reward for meeting targets

5. Involving *whanau* (extended family) in goal setting, achievement and organization of student learning to demonstrate a working *whanau* support system

6. Using a *hauora* (health and well-being) context to develop social and interpersonal skills

7. Emphasizing and encouraging the boys to use their bilingual talents in school and in off-site programmes

8. Using the whanau concept of the bilingual unit, and staff of the Maori department to help with science/*te reo* and holistic balance (Velde).

Language(s) of instruction

The language of instruction was English. This was for the Biology, Chemistry, Physics and Science teaching areas. The written instructions were in both Maori and English where possible. The school year is divided into quarters of ten weeks. The boys had one science teaching lesson per day. This daily lesson allowed for good continuity of the ideas and activities being covered in class.

The boys come from the Bilingual Department. This department has its own building and the boys have lessons in Maori for language and *takanga* (customs) daily. Science, however, had not been taught in this department. The nature of high-school science – with its practical work, use of chemicals and equipment, and complex language – had dictated its delivery in the Science department. This programme was thus the first attempt in our school to give our at-risk bilingual Maori students a specific science programme using Maori written instruction and contexts for the curriculum requirements, alongside a *hauora* programme to encourage student interest and achievement.

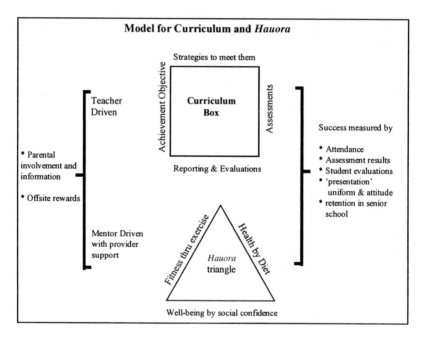

Model for Curriculum and *Hauora*

Curriculum/Themes

A *curriculum box/hauora triangle* model that incorporated the two methodologies (innovative teaching methods and motivational strategies) evolved over the years 1999 – 2002. The mentor-driven *hauora triangle* (see diagram above) was established to cope with the at-risk aspect of the students selected for the programme. It became a powerful tool and effectively drove the *curriculum box* (see diagram above). The curriculum box was established to ensure that every aspect of the curriculum delivery was relevant and user-friendly: Maori contexts (for achievement objectives), oral teaching with illustrations (avoiding text books), regular use of computers (for research, work presentation, working with graphics, and experiments), Maori instructions (tests and worksheets), work-related assessments (industry-based unit standards), and invited Maori speakers and other guests.

For example, the *New Zealand Education Department Curriculum Handbook: Achievement Objective* lists as an objective: 'Research and develop a defensible position about a selected issue affecting the NZ environment.' This objective has been taught within the context of *Te Ohu Kai mo Apopo* (Fishing for the Future). Fishing is a major part of Maori lifestyle. The following illustrates the unit structure for the *Te Ohu Kai mo Apopo*:

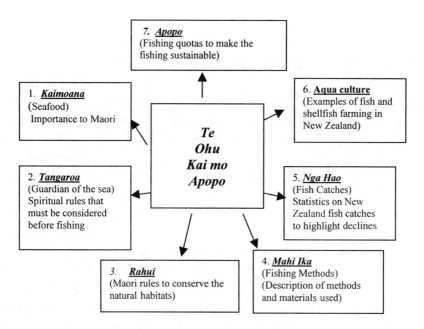

The science teachers were non-Maori. The mentors were all young high-achieving Maori men. The industry-based mentors from Fletcher Challenge Forests were already trained when they joined the programme in

Teachers

1999. The school mentors who joined in 2001 were advised by the programme director and the head of the Bilingual Department as to appropriate strategies to follow.

Materials and activities   The academic side of the programme has two main aspects: in-class curriculum work in contexts relevant to the Maori (such as fishing, flora and fauna), and applied work in forestry, food technology, electronics and computers to show science in action in the workplace. That applied work has included trips to Waikato Polytechnic and Fletcher Challenge Forests to build credits towards the National Certificate in Science level 2.

The *hauora* aspect includes swimming and gym training as well as mentoring and teaching about nutrition, relationships and parenting. It also includes off-site trips such as the Antarctic Centre in Christchurch, whale watching in Kaikoura and a visit to Te Papa in Wellington (Velde).

General Outcomes

Outcomes   The programme has achieved many of the objectives outlined in the original proposal. Students developed good routines for working on science projects and activities; the relevance of the science work motivated achievement; mentor support for goal-setting became an effective focusing tool. The school now has its first Forms 6 and 7 *Te Reo* science classes. Five students from the original 1999 Group 1 are in Form 8 this year. Two are sitting UB Science, two are taking Computer Certificate papers, and one is doing level three Forestry papers. The achievement of the boys in the programme has significantly changed the overall profile of Science as a subject area for boys in the bilingual department.

The programme has been innovative and well received by the boys, their *whanau* and their peers. Results and evaluations (now with the evaluation team in Auckland) support this. The curriculum/*hauora* model on which the programme is based has been shared with many other schools and Mrs Pani McLean (Head of Department, Maori) has answered many queries about the strategies used. At present, other departments in the school have not applied the model to their subject areas but they have been presented with a framework to consider. The curriculum aspect is easily transferable, but the *hauora* aspect needs to be individually adapted for each subject.

Measured Outcomes

The following pages provide a record of the strategies used to meet the objectives set out in the *Te Reo Putaiao* proposal. Previous full reports have provided measures on the 1 – 4 Output Performance Targets requested by the Ministry for the programme implementation.

Note that Group 1 (Bilingual) started in Form 5 in 1999 (as a trial), with seventeen students; Group 2 (Bilingual) started in Form 5 in 2001, with nineteen students; Group 3 (Mainstream) started in Form 4 in June 2001, with ten students. All groups are still operating in the school as of 2002.

Developing strategies to capture the imagination of at-risk *Te Reo* boys so that they will succeed in Science

1. Objective: To establish routines for student learning

Expected Outcomes:

*   Improved organization
*   Increased self-confidence.

Measured by:

*   Attendance in class (organization)
*   Continuing in Science (self-confidence)

- Sharing science understanding with *whanau* and friends.

Strategies used for improved organization:

- Students are provided with uniform and equipment, if necessary.
- Every student has a case-management folder in which they may store books and papers.
- Phone calls and visits to home, if necessary (but this is rarely necessary today).

Strategies used for increased self-confidence with science:

- Science ideas are taught orally alongside a large blackboard diagram.
- Formulae, key words, worked examples are built up around the visual model on the board.
- Textbooks are rarely used for reading. Textbook illustrations are used.
- The pitch of the lesson is simple and always start with a review.
- Computers are used consistently for experiments, graphing, mind maps, word processing and research.
- Students contributed to the design of a logo for class letterheads and worksheets.
- Students are encouraged to personalize their class work with relevant motifs/tags.
- Student worksheet instructions are written in Maori.
- Science topics are taught in a context relevant to Maori issues wherever possible.
- All issues (problems, class trips, parent visits) are discussed openly with HOD Maori and the course provider.
- Student learning is regularly done outside the classroom and driven by a *hauora* programme.
- All students, their work and their off-site trips,

are regularly photographed and built into a very visual class timeline.

- Parents receive regular newsletters about the programme and visit the school whare.

General Comments
The above strategies provided the boys with a routine which they could enjoy and relate to and which allowed them to concentrate on their learning. It minimized their barriers to learning (such as classroom walls, textbook reading, irrelevant science theory), used their strengths (oral and visual learning, relevant contexts, computers, open class forums for issues, a fitness regime) and provided them with an environment that was unthreatening (the programme was theirs and they could see a use for what they were learning).

2. Objective: To provide relevant contexts and technology-driven learning experiences

Expected Outcomes:

- Improved understanding of science ideas
- Qualifications (credits) towards NCEA (National Certificate of Educational Achievement) achieved
- Increased self-esteem with computer confidence.

Measured by:

- Curriculum Achievement
- Qualifications.

Strategies used for improved Science understanding:

- Iwi issues targeted in curriculum contexts, for example 'New Zealand's Unique Wild Life' (talk from Maori Arts & Crafts), 'Resource Management' (FCF Rainbow Mt) and 'Fishing'.
- Workforce opportunities targeted by using

industry-based contexts and by involving personnel from the industry, for example Forestry (Waiariki Institute of Technology and Fletcher Challenge Forests), Electronics (Waikato Polytechnic), and Food Technology (RBHS Staff).

• Work experience obtained through FCF mentors, for example tissue-culture lab, nursery and bush work.

Strategies used for increased computer confidence:

• Students do some writing or word processing regularly *every week*. The inability to transfer science understanding from 'mind' to 'paper' is a major barrier. Oral answers come easily; written ones require regular practice. Doing these on the computer removes the reluctance to write.

• Computers remove many of the barriers the boys have to achieving: they have spell-check for word processing, and programs to process and graph data (see below).

• Computer programs that accompany Robolab and Lego Technic have allowed the boys to learn simple programming instructions.

General Comments

Computers provide a real incentive for learning science. They remove the barriers associated with writing and calculating and provide the materials to draw, colour, create and present work creatively. The CNN footage of the September 11 tragedy, with the accompanying flight/ plane data, was used to teach the entire Form 6 physics unit on 'Forces & Motion'. E-mail contact was used for one year between FCF mentors and students. Two students are now in the RBHS Computer Academy.

3. Objective: To develop the setting of goals and the measures to reach them.

Expected Outcomes: Improved self-discipline in the school and in the classroom

Strategies Used:

- Goals are set at the start of each year and revisited regularly, with mentor support.
- The goals that are set target both school ambitions (for qualifications and success in the classroom) and community image ('looking sharp' and being fit).
- Goal-setting, measuring and relevant discussion are done outside the classroom (in a 'comfortable room').
- Classroom and *hauora* goals are driven by appropriate incentives, e.g. computer classes are given regularly for science activities, and fitness workouts are accompanied by breakfasts.
- The same incentives are offered on non-school days, and start at 8 am.
- Self-responsibility/discipline are encouraged by appropriate activities, for example: 8 am. start for *hauora*/computer programs; on trips, students are responsible for their own tickets and baggage; and rendezvous times on trips, as well as various files (for certificates, swim times, etc.) are student-maintained.
- Encouragement for achieving goals is provided not only by mentor, but also *hauora* and *whanau* support, class trips and activities and provider programmes.
- The mentor regularly visits the boys in class and works with them, particularly with Form 3 and 4 Maori mainstream students.

General Comments

Regularly revisiting set goals, and providing a mentoring environment in which the boys can achieve them, are good tools for encouraging achievement.

4. Objective: To introduce a Hauora Programme

Expected Outcomes:

Improved:
*   fitness
*   health awareness
*   interpersonal skills
*   parenting skills.

Measured by:

*   swimming time trials
*   health sessions
*   provider programmes.

Strategies used for fitness:

*   The fitness programme involves swimming for aerobic fitness and weights for strength. A one-hour (8 – 9 am) session is scheduled for each week. This is mentor-assisted.
*   Each term, fitness data is loaded into the computer by the students and graphed to display their progress. This is mentor-assisted.

Strategies used for health:

*   Health awareness is targeted after each exercise by relevant explanations.
*   Breakfast after the swim programme targets diet. It is healthy and prepared especially for the boys. *Whanau* have assisted with breakfasts.
*   One day a week is identified as a 'looking after ourselves' day. It coincides with fitness swim/gym day. Students are encouraged to eat sensibly, avoid smoking and drinking alcohol.

Strategies used for provider programme:

- Interpersonal skills targeted by a six-week programme. It allows the boys to practise social skills for specific occasions, such as job interviews, and looking after girlfriends, sisters and mothers.
- Parenting skills targeted by a ten-week programme. Rotorua has high statistics for teenage pregnancies and the programme used this as a focus.

General Comments

The *hauora* component of the science programme has been hugely successful. Both parent and student evaluations praise this aspect. It has effectively driven the curriculum delivery of the programme with its 'newness' and relevance.

5. Objective: To provide high-impact offsite experiences.

Expected Outcomes:

- To widen experiences beyond the local comfort zone.
- To introduce real, rather than virtual, science learning experiences.
- To encourage leadership in unfamiliar situations.

General Comments:

- Trips outside the classroom were rewards. Some were local, others were designed to provide learning experiences the boys would never forget.
- The trips created situations that made the boys take on new responsibilities – such as *Marae* (Maori community meeting place) welcomes and farewells, listening to 'lectures', providing support for their peers, budgeting their daily 'meal

money', looking after their baggage and tickets, signing themselves in on flights and buses.

• The trips away from the Rotorua comfort zone also provided opportunities for all students to show unseen skills/talents: thank-you speeches, group leadership, map-reading, budgeting and keeping track of their belongings.

• All trips are 'heavily photographed'. The photos are built into displays around the lab and are magnets for all Maori boys who visit the lab. They act as a constant reminder of the learning experiences. Many boys requested copies of the photos to share with *whanau* at Christmas.

Lessons learnt: strengths and weaknesses

The programme has also provided challenges. The small size of classes (<20) requires a high teacher/student ratio. Composite classes have not been easy to timetable. The complexity and holistic approach of the programme makes it difficult for a single provider to maintain and oversee. Costs for the essential *hauora* programmes are high, and it has taken awhile to adapt the mentor programme to our needs.

The original programme and budget framework outlined in the proposal have been slightly modified over the last three years. This has been necessary for a variety of reasons: providers become unavailable (i.e. for the visit to Leigh marine reserve); the FCF mentor programme changed when FCF underwent a major restructuring process; the retention of many of the boys into senior science meant the programme was financing more boys and programmes than planned. The introduction of the *hauora* model into Years 9 and 10 mainstream classes to support at-risk Maori students increased the workload. In addition, the time allocation for recording all the evaluation data requested was grossly underestimated. Some of the evaluation forms sent by the Auckland University team for the boys to complete were at an inappropriate reading level and the changes requested in the data collection format, midway through the programme, caused frustrations.

Implementing the programme has been a real challenge. Many Maori students at risk of educational underachievement are able but have found the barriers to traditional achievement in schools too great. The strategies that have been used to reduce these barriers have allowed many of these students to find achievement an enjoyable challenge and worth staying at school to work towards.

1999 – 2002 Trial Period. The school is keen to reintroduce the programme. This will happen when the Ministry of Education reviews their funding allocations to schools for 'Students at Risk'. There are a number of schools still trialling 'At Risk' programmes and these will need to be evaluated by the Ministry before they make their funding decisions.

Duration

'Innovations Funding Pool for Students at Risk' from the Ministry of Education, and computer technology from Ngati Whakaue Endowment Trust Board.

Funding/Budget

Rotorua Boys' High School

Responsible organization(s) and institution(s)

I wish to thank the Ministry of Education for financial support; Pani McLean for her unending encouragement; Fletcher Challenge Forests for allowing us to participate in their mentor programme; Ngati Whakaue for funding the Science Bundles and Robolab technologies; Ann Brimmer for all the data input and collation; and, lastly, the boys themselves. They were prepared to 'give hard work a go'.

Janet Nairn
Rotorua Boy's High School
Pukuatua Street
Rotorua
New Zealand
Tel: + 64 7 348 6169

Contact

Fax. + 64 7 346 1270
E-mail: science@rotoruaboyshigh.school.nz

Janet Nairn is director of the programme.

Additional information has been quoted, where indicated, from the article, 'A time for togs', by Matt Velde, in the *Edgazette*, retrieved from: http://www.edgazette. govt.nz/articles/show_articles.cgi

PERU:
'THE ASHANINKA CREATORS':
AN EXPERIENCE
FROM THE PERSPECTIVE
OF INDIGENOUS EDUCATION
Walter Heredia Martínez

Non-formal education: an educational experience for children, youth, adults and elders, connected to a process of community and local development.

Type of programme and educational level

Six communities living in the river basins of the Tambo, Perené and Satipo rivers in the high rain forests of the Department of Junín in Central Amazonian region, Peru.

Geographic and administrative aspects

The Ashaninka communities

Indigenous target groups

What we describe here is a fully articulated educational programme – connected to a process of community and local development in the Central Amazonian region of Peru. Here, we are working jointly with the communities of the Ashaninka people and with the Programme for the Promotion and Capacity-Building in the Amazon (PROCAM).

Programme description

Summary

Interventions are both community-based and cultural in character, drawing on the participation of children, youth, adults and the elderly of both sexes in six communities of the Tambo, Perené and Satipo rivers, located in the Department of Junín in the high rain forests of the Central Amazonian region.

The educational programme has emerged and evolved from the deepest roots of the Ashaninka culture and people. By this we mean 'indigenous education' – an education grounded in the roots of the Ashaninka's own identity and sustained through interaction and communication (around similarities and differences) with other cultures in the rich, diverse and multi-ethnic mosaic of Peru (a country with seventy-two ethno-linguistic peoples within its borders). This type of education is also born out of dialogue and dialectic confrontation with universal culture.

Background: legal-political, socio-economic and linguistic situation

The Ashaninka people are the largest population group in the Central Amazonian region of Peru and one of most numerous in the whole of the continental Amazonian river basin. They belong to the linguistic family Arawak, whose official number is 61,140, and who can be found living in 346 rural communities in the Peruvian central rain forest.

In their distant and recent history, the Ashaninka have shared many of the same fundamental problems and difficulties as many other indigenous population groups on the South American continent.

Given the scope of the present study, we will restrict ourselves to a brief summary of these:

- Economic neocolonialism
- Cultural homogenization
- Juridical fragility
- War and militarization.

During the 1989–93 period, the political violence in Peru left some 4,000 Ashaninka dead and 10,000 displaced from their communities.

Since 1998, a team from PROCAM (itself multi-disciplinary and multi-ethnic in composition) has been working towards a process of sustainable local development and empowerment for these communities. Through dialogue between different knowledge systems and a campaign of concerted and complementary activities with the Ashaninka themselves, three interlinked and strategic lines of action have emerged: Culture, Education, and Integrated Development.

Under the umbrella of PROCAM, the 'Ashaninka Creators' component has been implemented since 2002 within a framework and perspective of indigenous education. The approach is self-sustaining and representative of the essential links or connections through which the Ashaninka people construct their belief systems, as well as their views on reality, human beings and the world.

Unlike many other approaches, however, the educational process has been conceived to foster learning that is endogenous to the Ashaninka people and their culture. It is not segmented, parcelled or 'systemic'. Nor is it limited to space or time. Instead, it has been aligned to all fields and dimensions of life, both past and present.

Similarly, the educational process is neither borrowed nor imported from any one theoretical education approach or focus. It has been elaborated from the experience of 'living' and 'being' an Ashaninka, or the very foundations of their cultural identity. It summons the totality of the dimensions by which the Ashaninka (like many other indigenous peoples of the continent) construct and reconstruct their individual and collective being. As such, it refers to the totality of their intellectual, affective, physical and spiritual capacities and competencies.

The process generated by the programme is helping to strengthen the cultural identity of the Ashaninka people. It does so by promoting and developing the integrity of their cultural capacities and practices – whether they be artistic, social, economic or ecological. In themselves, these are the basic elements for the exercise of the Ashaninka's human and democratic rights. At the same time, the programme is helping to raise ethnic self-esteem, which is important in the struggle against poverty and in efforts to stimulate community development.

The framework for the programme also grew out of an evaluation of, and critical reflection upon:

- the impact of existing educational policies on indigenous peoples in Latin America
- the contributions and limitations of current theories of intercultural bilingual education.

Based on these critical assessments, a pedagogical vision of what is implied by 'indigenous education' was then elaborated.

'Ashaninka Creators' represents a concrete attempt to holistically recover what we assume to be indigenous education in its various forms and dimensions – as an option and practice for the teaching-learning process, as an educational model and as a pedagogic strategy.

But in trying to define the framework for such an integrated education programme, it was also necessary to draw on the basic tenets of the science of education. Since learning is sustained in an explicit or implicit way through different theoretical and cultural platforms, critical reflection was needed at every step of designing the educational approach, so that the vision of education corresponded to the different knowledge-based and epistemological realities of the people in the target communities, both as human beings and in terms of human learning.

Objectives and focus Then, what do we mean by indigenous education? In general, the term refers to the essential characteristics of a particular type of educational process through which our people and indigenous civilizations have evolved and still survive on our continent. In this sense, indigenous education comprises a qualitatively different form of education, one which has evolved through a particular

universe of educational phenomenon and human experiences.

As such, indigenous education synthesizes a combination of concrete, diverse, isolated and singular
actions that are present and developed in the educational
practices of our cultures. It includes the essential and
fundamental notions that characterize the Ashaninka
people and that allow one to identify its fundamental
rules and values. The totality is usually expressed in the
three connected and converging world views of the
Andean, Amazonian and Mesoamerican cultures:

- as societies which interacted and still interact with
  their environment in a holistic, integral, cosmos-
  centric way
- as human beings who accepted and still accept
  themselves through their ways of life and of being,
  whether this refers to human, natural, or cosmic
  relationships
- as bearers of wisdom or knowledge, sustained in
  relations between rational consciousness, tran-
  scendental consciousness and the Unity of Being,
  Knowing, Feeling and Doing.

Departing from this educational vision and model,
'Ashaninka Creators' proposes to:

- Strengthen and enhance the artistic-cultural
  capacities and practices of the Ashaninka people
  by generating collective spaces for cultural recovery and creativity, which at the same time
  constitute learning spaces for the promotion and
  stimulation of local community development.

With this in mind, the programme has been implemented with the main objective of recovering the different
elements of the educational-cultural process through
which the Ashaninka people have evolved. That is to

say, their vision of the universe from their own knowledge-based, epistemological and pedagogic foundations.

Participation

The programme began with information days and consultation meetings in each Ashaninka community with a focus on two related thematic axes:

1. A comprehensive and detailed explanation of the objectives, activities and results of the programme, as well as the resources and budget.
2. An assessment of the current status of the cultural and artistic practices of the Ashaninka people, as well as identification of experts and teachers in each of the artistic disciplines.

These information days permitted the selection and organization of group leaders, elders and artists in each community. They also provided an opportunity to carry out an assessment from the perspective of the Ashaninka people themselves.

Methods used

The workshops generated open and collective spaces for the recovery of cultural practices and disciplines as well as opportunities for strengthening intergenerational bonds between children, adolescents, youth and adults of both sexes.

The programme has led to a process of intra-culturality; by this we mean greater synergies within the world of the Ashaninka people. Cultural relationships have been strengthened among Ashaninka, as individuals, families, communities and among their community organizations. In this way, the programme is contributing to an improvement and strengthening of indigenous institutions, with the active participation of women.

The programme has also played an important role in renewing pride in the culture and identity of the Ashaninka people in the local and regional spheres. This was faciliated by the organization of a multidisciplinary artistic show of the Ashaninka people in the city of

Satipo (capital of the province of the same name), which drew a massive crowd of the local population, with around 15,000 people attending.

The preparation and organization of the show generated an innovatory space for intercultural dialogue between the Ashaninka people and local civil society. Since a high level of consultation and a number of alliances were needed, particularly involving local institutions and government, the show provided an opportunity to raise awareness of the values and customs of the Ashaninka people, thereby increasing recognition of their cultural heritage within the wider society.

Using non-formal educational methods targeting children, youth, adults and community elders (both men and women) , the programme has helped to generate open and collective spaces for the recovery and re-creation of cultural practices and linkages in the diverse dimensions of their daily life – whether in relation to production or re-production in the material or spiritual fields.

Two educational modalities were employed: the educational information days, and workshops for artistic-cultural recovery and re-creation. Because of their wide experience in acting and theatre training using different techniques and methods, the Association 'Artistica Cuatro Tablas' was asked to contribute to programme implementation. As a result, the programme has been able to draw on the services of professional artists who, because of their own background and development path, are able to relate to the spirit of the programmes. The use of different techniques has facilitated the possibility of drawing out innate Ashaninka qualities and capacities from their daily practices and rituals.

In the development of the education programme, the Ashaninka stressed that communication through the language of the body, of dreams, intuitions, affections, feelings and instincts should be at least as important as communication through the language of words (constructed with ideas, concepts and meanings).

Language(s) of instruction

Both Ashaninka and Spanish were used as the languages of communication during the information days and workshops. This often involved using key concepts which where then developed further in the original language. These advanced ways of communicating allowed teaching and learning to take place in a more energetic and holistic fashion.

Curriculum/Themes

Both the informational meetings and the workshops took place in spaces for communication and exchange, drawing on contributions from and between members of the Ashaninka community. This permitted the educational process to be based on the Ashaninka's own perception and vision of thematic areas and programme contents, such as the following:

- The fundamental bases and principals of the Ashaninka worldview
- The fundamental bases of individual and collective identity and self-esteem – or what it means to be Ashaninka
- The Ashaninka's own perception and definition of what is presumed to be 'Ashaninka culture'
- The rediscovery of ancestral cultural practices and the current status of artistic-cultural practices
- The identification of knowledge, techniques and skills involved in diverse artistic cultural practices
- Identification of production processes and the main components of socio-educational and cultural practices
- Identification and analysis of the main factors which threaten their cultural identity, as well as those that strengthen and enhance it
- Recognition and organization of the main educational and cultural agents

- Collective recovery and re-creation of knowledge and practices linked to: the protection and balanced exploitation of eco-systems; the management and organization of territorial space; social, political and cultural organizations and institutions, and the bases of Ashaninka leadership.

Teachers

Elders (men and women), as well as others knowledgeable about ancestral practices, were the main teachers during programme implementation, as were young leaders committed to the recovery and re-creation of artistic cultural disciplines. They developed a dialogue and exchanged knowledge with the team of facilitators from PROCAM, as well as with the artists from the theatre group of the Cuatrotablas Association.

Activities and materials

The education process was elaborated from didactic methods that were taken from the processes used by the Ashaninka themselves in the creation and re-creation of music, dance, theatre, myths and stories, weaving, and handicrafts, as well as hunting, fishing, gathering and the management of their forests and natural resources.

The workshops permitted Ashaninka learners and teachers from different communities, of both sexes and all ages, to be mobilized for set periods of time in the teaching and learning process as it relates to distinct cultural and artistic disciplines and practices.

In this way, music, dance, Ashaninka theatre, artisan and weaver groups were gathered, which, aside from acting as cultural ambassadors, were also leaders of community development due to their knowledge of the forests, the organization of the territory and management of biodiversity.

Outcomes

The programme has led to a process of intra-culturality; by this we mean greater synergies within the society and world of the Ashaninka people. The programme has been able to draw on their knowledge, values and behaviours, while mobilizing and aligning their cultural and artistic competencies and capacities to their needs – and perceptions of the future – as a people. The programme is thus founded on the fundamental components of their vision of the universe and their identity as an indigenous people.

The process generated by the programme has been a mobilizing force in raising consciousness and pride in their ethnic identity, while creating spaces for reflection on what it means to be an Ashaninka. This has led to changes in behaviours and attitudes of the participants, who now recognize the value of their own cultural identity. At the same time, the programme has helped to broaden the understanding of the cultural and political role that the Ashaninka perform as protagonists not only in their own territories, but also in larger territorial spaces and contexts, such as the region and the country.

In this way, parallel and convergent synergies with other cultural groups (Andean and coastal populations), social actors and institutions are emerging in the local and regional spheres, thereby creating the possibility of new and more stable intercultural relationships.

The programme made possible the organization of the multidisciplinary artistic show of the Ashaninka people in one of the region's main cities (Satipo). It was a historic event in that it provided an opportunity to raise awareness of Ashaninka artistic capacities, whether they be in the area of theatre, music, dance, stories, handicrafts or textiles, while raising awarenss of the economic, social, political and cultural rights of the Ashaninka people.

Lessons learnt: strengths and weaknesses

From a pedagogical point of view, in as much as the model of indigenous education originates and evolves from a systematic and holistic approach based on indigenous knowledge systems, epistemology and pedagogy, and overcomes piecemeal, reductionist or unilateral conceptions of culture and education, it is helping to widen the horizons of what we understand by indigenous culture and constitutes a valid pedagogic focus for the whole society and not only 'for indigenous people'.

Indigenous education should be accepted as an educational approach for all those who seek to construct a sustainable and unified society. For this to happen, conventional conceptions of intercultural bilingual education as being 'for indigenous people' – and which are limited to the linguistic aspect – need to become a thing of the past. Indigenous education should not be viewed as a pedagogic modality for 'minorities', isolated and excluded from the rest of the educational system. For such limited approaches result in programmes that are pedagogically and socially impracticable and unsustainable.

In short, the model of indigenous education and its educational strategy constitute a pedagogic alternative with a scientific basis in, and for, societies characterized by their multicultural and intercultural realities.

1st Phase: June 2002 July 2003	**Duration**
Winning Project of the National Contest of Innovative Projects 'Creators of Culture', Peru 2002, funded by Ventana de la Sociedad Civil (Window of Civil Society) – the World Bank. Funds received: US$21,000. Kellog Foundation: US$5,000.	**Funding/Budget**
Team for Promotion and Capacity-Building in the Amazon – PROCAM	**Responsible institution(s)**
Walter Heredia Martínez Presidente Consejo Directivo PROCAM Jirón Ayacucho 212 Magdalena del Mar Lima Peru Telefax: 00511 4630647	**Contact**

E-mail: procam@amauta.rcp.net.pe
kantatayta@hotmail.com

Notes and References:

Lazo, Machado J. *La educación como función social general.*
Sucre, Bolivia: Universidad San Francisco Xavier, 1999.

PERU:
REVALUING AND USING
HERBAL MEDICINE
FROM THE ANDEAN REGION
Noé Miguel Chávez Velazquez

Rural and Environmental Education: formal primary education (7 – 11 years)

Type of programme and educational level

Cusco, Peru

Geographic and administrative aspects

Pupils and community: students from Quechua-speaking communities, many of whom are migrants from the rural areas in the provinces of Cusco, Apurímac and Madre de Dios, as well as children from bilingual families living in urban areas.

Indigenous target groups

This case study describes the experiences of a school workshop programme in Peru on herbal and medicinal plants and on using biodiversity in a sustainable way.

Description of programme

This school programme has permitted students to exchange and share information on the use of local plants with their families and relatives. Thematic areas have now been incorporated into the curriculum after testing in various rural and urban schools in the Cusco area.

Between 1995 and 1996, different types of native vegetation were collected from the Kachimayu river basin and planted on the school terraces as part of efforts

Summary

to conserve the area's biodiversity. Students from the Third, Fourth and Fifth Grades (8 – 10 years old) used their knowledge, skills and attitudes about nature conservation to seed, water, cultivate and harvest these plants.

Many of these plants are now being transformed into useful and durable vegetal products such as herbal teas, creams, medicinal syrups and essential oils. Students develop an understanding and empathy with nature as a vital part of their basic education. They are taught how to recognize different types of vegetation using their own senses: smelling, touching and studying the external features of the plants. Classroom theory is reinforced through practice in natural surroundings, permitting closer contact with the environment.

Educational and social context

Background: legal-political, socio-economic and linguistic situation

In the past, and even today, the peoples of Cusco have placed great importance on aromatic and medicinal plants found in their region. But the influence of consumerism and other Western cultural patterns are increasingly influential. And we are losing our ancestral knowledge, the cultural values and the wisdom of our peoples. Yet although education has lost out in this regard it is still possible to tap into the knowledge of older generations through consultation.

Institutional context

Since 1981, the 'Pukllasunchis' Association has been concerned with generating frameworks for educational transformation within the public education system. These programmes are intended for the direct benefit of marginalized peoples in the urban areas of Cusco. In the past few years, programmes have also been extended to children, youth and families living in rural areas surrounding the city, especially those vulnerable to social, cultural and economic marginalization.

'Pukllasunchis Primary School' is a pilot project with a difference. The aim is to include productive activities in the academic timetable/curriculum. The school is located in the city of Cusco in the district of San Sebastian, situated in the lower basin of the Kachimayu River at 3,300 metres above sea level in North-East Peru. Native vegetation and flora can still be found in the upper area of the basin, while a dense area of bio-diversity has been identified on the banks of the Kachimayu river, where many medicinal and herbal plants grow.

Pukllasunchis School and the Institute of Ecology and Medicinal Plants (IEPLAM) have been leading efforts to legally protect this area for educational and recreational purposes and in promotion of eco-tourism. Some communities have even started *in situ* protection of plant biodiversity to combat erosion. Native plants were collected from the Kachimayu and replanted in school gardens between 1995 and 1996 as an example of bio-diversity conservation taking place at source.

How did the programme originate?
Work on the programme began following the carrying out of a similar experience by IAPLA, an international organization, based on the extraction of essential oils from aromatic and medicinal plants. The idea was to replicate this experience for the primary school students. The programme is innovative in that student activities revolve around the cultivation and conservation of native plant matter, leading to the development of handmade products and the sale of natural medicines.

It must be highlighted, however, that the management of waste products in the district of San Sebastian has affected the level of biodiversity in the area and created contamination. Meanwhile, natural landslides have washed away much of the biomass. The district of San Sebastian is therefore very much depleted, and many of the medicinal plants are left untouched as their use is inappropriate.

The objectives are:

Objectives and focus

- to recover traditional wisdom related to native vegetation for medicinal and nutritional use
- to enhance the school curriculum by introducing thematic areas related to biodiversity (knowledge, attitudes and values), and
- to develop youth capacities towards future productive activities.

Specific aims

- To sensitize and raise awareness of the need for planned and appropriate extraction of natural resources towards sustainable production.
- To recover, preserve, conserve and optimize the value of natural resources.
- To improve the knowledge, capacities and technical skills of the students of Puklla, through the development of a systematic perspective.
- To encourage the rational and appropriate use of medicinal natural resources.
- To produce natural products with minimum negative spillovers and promote eco-consciousness in the productive workshops of the school.
- To equip the school with capacities guaranteeing the sustainability of the project.

Participation

The 'Pukllasunchis Primary School' project has been designed for the children and youth of the marginalized urban areas of the city of Cusco. Rural communities are not directly targeted. The students' parents have participated in project planning through regular consultation meetings and workshops where pedagogical principles were reflected upon and discussed. Teachers then took their contributions and conclusions and incorporated them into the curricular activities of the school.

In addition, the Assembly of Parents follows up on observations and comments made by families and parents in conjunction with the teachers' co-ordination team. The comments are responded to via a special bulletin and/or organized workshops or conversations directly with the stakeholders.

- Launch of a productive workshop for primary level (1997)
- Establishment of an independent area (1999).

Methods used

The project was included in the school programming and timetable. Boys and girls in Second, Third, Fourth and Fifth Grades at primary level (7 to 11 year-olds) participated. Teachers from the fields of Natural Science and Social Science worked together to elaborate the contents of the framework for the workshop in light of the knowledge, skills, attitudes and values for each of the grades of the primary curriculum.

The school set aside a small fund to purchase basic equipment (drainage equipment, an electronic scale, a propane heater, basic agricultural tools, a computer and printer) as well as various other materials. Likewise the school provides a basic laboratory for workshop activities. Each grade works in groups of ten students.

Since 1997, surveys and interviews with professionals, volunteers and community elders have been undertaken to compile data, and documents have been updated to include information on the locality.

IEPLAM prepares teacher training courses focusing on Andean aromatic and medicinal plants. Since 1988, experts from Pukllasunchis have been carrying out a study in the river basin, which has been translated into Spanish for dissemination in urban schools of the Quecha area.

Project activities attempt to respect the skills range of each age group and are complemented by practical tasks in Natural and Social Sciences classes. These include:

Curriculum/Themes

Skills

- The ability to carry out experiments using the senses and comparing findings with other students.
- Undertaking interviews with settlers of nearby areas regarding the use of aromatic and medicinal plants.
- Using specimens to study plant morphology and physiology and to describe their natural habitat.
- Developing practical skills in a laboratory setting or in the field.
- Harvesting aromatic and medicinal plants following the cycle of the moon.
- Making compost for improving soil quality.
- Using natural fertilizers without the use of chemicals.
- Distinguishing between exotic and native plants and assessing the costs and benefits of each.
- Working in groups with various responsibilities at the same time.
- Developing and using communication and production (labelling and selling) skills.
- Making decisions and holding opinions.
- Preparing products following basic scientific methods, rules and instructions.
- Identifying plants of the locality using basic biological criteria.
- Carrying out experiments for biological pest control; trial and error.

Attitudes

- To have a respectful attitude towards nature when collecting and using plants.
- To optimize valuable materials and resources while using them.

- To maintain a co-operative attitude while developing a productive activity.
- To recognize the wisdom of elder family members or settlers with knowledge of plants and nature.
- To search for alternative locations near the school as a part of efforts to replicate the experience and expand the project in the community.
- To compare the natural and urban environment and understand the values of each.
- To design a new set of alternative products creatively.

Concepts

- To research the aromatic and medicinal qualities of plants.
- To learn about biodiversity in nearby landscapes, observing animals, insects and other invertebrates.
- To study biodiversity among wild vegetation and soils outside the classroom in order to understand soil types, air quality, water sources and their relation with living creatures and the cycle of nature.
- To deal with and develop new types of organic crop cultivation from a theoretical and practical standpoint.
- To apply theoretical concepts during laboratory or field work.
- To learn aseptic practices in the preparation of medicines and food.
- To practice mathematic calculations of weight, measurements and selling.
- To have a holistic and systematic perspective of the school environment and society.

The school has overcome obstacles and conflicts:

- By carrying out cleaning-up campaigns to avoid the growth of contaminated crops in the gardens.

- By carrying out activities using costly laboratory equipment among the older students.
- By acquiring sanitary authorizations and certificates.
- Through the zeal of the specialists in spite of the lack of instruction.
- Through promotion and incentive to research for our medicinal resources in the school.

Language(s) of instruction

Cusco is situated in a Quechua-speaking Andean area. In the urban areas where our centre is located, the daily use of this language is being lost. The first language of our students is Spanish, but the school teaches Quechua as second language as part of our efforts to increase the use of this language and promote positive attitudes towards it. The school also seeks recognition of the language's importance within our ancestral culture.

Teachers/Training

The majority of teachers are young people from Cusco who have been trained at local teacher training colleges and/or at the San Antonio Abad University of Cusco. One of the most important qualities sought is the ability to work in a team. Once they become members of our institution, the teachers therefore receive ongoing training to raise their professional and personal skills levels.

Activities and materials

The project works with the active participation of the school community to promote the appropriate use of natural resources. Students develop a broad overview of the natural environment and its cycles, leading to more sustainable exploitation of its resources. Educational outdoor activities are programmed for seeding, watering, fertilizing and harvesting aromatic and medicinal plants. The plants are then transformed into useful, long-life vegetal products, such as herbal teas, rubbing creams, medicinal syrups and freshly extracted essential oils.

Outcomes

The project has been carried out since 1997. More than ninety students and teachers per year have learned about biodiversity and have acquired skills in related productive activities. Currently, eight school gardens (covering a total area of around 350 m^2) are being planted with native plants and certain exotic aromatic and medicinal plants.

Pukllasunchis organizes an open market every two months during the academic year, during which the students get a chance to sell their produce to the general public and tourists. The school also uses this opportunity to display the project to neighbours of the San Blas area in Cusco.

The project has also been linked to other activities such as the sorting and recycling of waste and the development of management systems for natural plant cycles.

Lessons learnt: strengths and weaknesses

To date, more than 400 photographs have been taken to identify the flora of the Kachimayu area. These are being classified for publication as a primary-school text.

Based on their theoretical understanding, the students are now able to recognize natural vegetation using their senses and have developed an empathy for nature. This project has also facilitated the fluent exchange of information among their family members on the use of plants, thereby improving relationships within the community.

It is crucial to promote the consumption of local products as sources of proteins and vitamins, and thus avoid their replacement – because they are believed to be 'less civilized' – by more Western products, a trend that increases malnutrition and leads to loss of cultural identity and self-esteem.

Working on thematic areas related to biodiversity is a pilot experience that can be considered for replication. The students can directly see the relevance of existing plant biodiversity and its relation to their quality of life. This provides students with a direct experience on issues of biodiversity at the global level.

Culture and traditional knowledge are being recovered through scientific information gathered at the beginning of the research. All the thematic areas have been incorporated into the curriculum following validation for future replication in rural and urban schools.

By teaching children from an early age in formal, non-formal and informal settings, the experience of environmental education might help to avoid the future destruction of the natural environment, while promoting respect, justice, co-operation, diversity, harmony and transcendence.

When pupils get involved, they get to know and love biodiversity. They will talk about it with adults and learn to respect it. Then they will guard and value it, and ultimately they will be able to conserve it.

The workshops have demonstrated their importance in raising awareness of the traditional use of aromatic and medicinal plants in the school community and among the wider population. By optimizing the use of scarce resources of the area, the programme is continuing to contribute to the meeting of basic human needs.

Duration

Since 1996

Funding/Budget

The Education Centre is partially financed by parents through contributions which are determined according to family income. Economic, social and cultural heterogeneity are important elements of our framework. We also receive support from the Ministry of Education (which has granted some teacher posts) and we still rely on individual contributions as well as those from Swiss institutions.

Responsible institution(s)

Pukllasunchis School, with contributions from the European Economic Community (Cooperation for International Development [CID]) and the Pukllasunchis Association.

Contact

Noé Miguel Chávez Velasques
Casilla Postal: 776

Cusco
Peru
Tel: + 51 84-237918
E-mail: pukllas@pukllasunchis.org
Website: http://www.pukllasunchis.org

Notes and References:

Juan Diego López-Giraldo, Caterina Cárdenas, Noé Miguel Chávez, Ingrid Salcedo and Yda Torreblanca, 'An experience for learning Andean biodiversity contents included on the elementary school curriculum', http://www.iubs.org/cbe/pdf/lopez_g.pdf

RUSSIAN FEDERATION: THE RUSSIAN INDIGENOUS TRAINING CENTRE (RITC) [1]

RITC and INRIPP

Type of programme and educational level

RITC offers training courses to post-secondary individuals, with the aim of preparing Russia's indigenous communities for the challenges they face in making the transition to a market economy.

Geographical and administrative level

The RITC head office is currently based in Moscow, with one branch office established in the Taimyr region of Northern Siberia. Additional branch offices are currently being negotiated in the Khanty-Mansyisk, Yamalo-Nenets and Evenkyia regions, in which indigenous communities are located.

Indigenous target groups

There are forty different indigenous groups living in Russia, totalling approximately 210,000 people. RITC targets active representatives of these groups – from Siberia, the Far North and Far East of the Russian Federation – who are willing to contribute to the economic and sustainable development of their people at the community and regional levels.

Description of programme

Summary

The Russian Indigenous Training Centre was established in the year 2000 with the primary goal of offering training courses to stimulate community economic development. Initially it offered two courses: the Community Economic Development Officers (CEDO) training course, and the Regional Economic Development Officers (REDO) training course. Those who participate in the REDO course then become 'outreach officers' for the region in which their community is located and are responsible for identifying and developing projects that lead to revenue generation. They are assisted in their work by the 'Outreach Department' of RITC.

CEDO: training for Community Economic Development Officers
The course is held once a year, for thirteen to sixteen participants, selected according to set criteria and an equal representation of nationalities, regions and gender. This is a two-week course currently offered at the Moscow site, but will also be offered at the branch sites when they are established.

REDO: training for Regional Economic Development Officers
The course is held once a year for five to six participants selected according to set criteria and an equal representation of nationalities, regions and gender. This course is five to six weeks in length, and training currently takes place in Russia and Canada. The theoretical portion of the course is delivered in Moscow, or at a branch site, and is followed by an illustrative tour of aboriginal communities in Canada.

The criteria used to select candidates for these courses are predominately related to the individuals' involvement in their communities and economic activities, as opposed to their educational background. Interestingly, over 50 per cent of those who apply to these courses have a university degree.

RITC's course curricula and programmes for workshops and seminars have been steadily expanding and now incorporate more topics of interest and importance to Russia's indigenous peoples on such issues as co-management, land and resources, environmental protection, and legislation. Manuals are produced for each of the training courses and these are given to the participants, to be kept as reference material once they have returned to their home communities.

Background: legal-political, socio-economic, educational and linguistic situation

The indigenous population (which is currently about 1 per cent of the total Russian population) of the Russian North has been severely impacted by the political and socio-economic developments that have taken place in the Russian Federation over the past decade. The reform process has resulted in the demise of the centralized subsidy and supply systems and of the social safety net, which has led to further 'marginalization' of the Northern Indigenous peoples. For example, their nominal income is only one half to one third of the Russian average, their birth rate decreased by 69 per cent between 1990 and 1996 while the death rate rose 35.5 per cent. During development of the oil, gas and mineral resources of the Russian North little heed was given to renewable resources upon which indigenous peoples depended, with the result that some indigenous people lost the skills needed for effective hunting, fishing, trapping and gathering. Unemployment rates are as high as 60 per cent in some indigenous communities; the rate of alcoholism in Northern communities is 12 to 14 times the Russian average; and the incidence of tuberculosis is 2.5 to 10 times higher in indigenous communities (taken from 'Northern Statistics: Spine Chilling', Rossiyskaya Gazeta, 27 February 1999).

At the same time, the North represents an area of vital economic importance for the Russian Federation. It accounts for one fifth of Russia's Gross Domestic Product and about 60 per cent of the raw material exports from Russia. The North also accounts for over half of all the fish and seafood harvested in Russia. The North of the Russian Federation ought to be the place where life is good. Instead, the lack of employment, the exorbitant cost of living, and the difficulties of maintaining steady access to the most basic food products, medicines and fuel are painful realities of Northern living, especially from the indigenous perspective. Educational opportunities are diminishing for indigenous people, and their own languages are under constant threat as diminution in traditional spheres of economic activity reduces indigenous language usage sharply.

The *strategic objectives of the Centre* are to:

Objectives and focus

- provide training that integrates and supports the traditional economies of the indigenous communities
- provide personnel training, retraining and advanced training to foster an entrepreneurship culture and social activism
- bring interns together with the aim of shaping a culture of corporate entrepreneurship and of finding, together, solutions to social and economic challenges
- promote the Centre's ideas at the regional level through the creation of branch offices, thereby establishing a regional network.

The *tactical objectives of the Centre* during its initial stage of development are aimed chiefly at accomplishing the above strategic objectives, and include the following:

- developing the structure of its educational programmes (economic, legal, social, environmental, sustainable development, etc.)
- providing methodological support for educational programmes
- establishing a mobile team of highly professional instructors
- developing and testing intern-selection procedures

- devising mechanisms to assess training efficiency and to obtain feedback from interns
- developing principles and arrangements for fee-based training
- providing information support for educational programmes
- creating an enabling environment in the regions, by encouraging good community/government/company relations.

Participation

Prior to the establishment of RITC, a 'field mission' was undertaken to identify opportunities and challenges for economic development in indigenous communities of Northern Russia. The field mission team travelled to the Kamchatka Peninsula and the Khabarovsk Territory, which were selected as being representative of the far northern and southern part of the Russian North. Following a series of meetings with many individuals and government representatives in several indigenous communities, the field mission identified 'needs', 'opportunities' and 'challenges' faced by these communities and then went on to make recommendations for 'training priorities' and 'selection criteria' for potential candidates. Using this information, RITC established its aims and objectives and identified its initial training priorities.

The Russian Association of Indigenous Peoples of the North, Far East and Siberia (RAIPON) approved the concept and the Centre was established.

Participation in the courses offered by RITC is through an open application process organized to reach the indigenous audience through the RITC website www.csipn.ru, the RAIPON website www.raipon.org, the 'World of Indigenous Peoples' magazine published by RAIPON, and the RITC Newsletter mailed out to all the regional associations of indigenous peoples, to all key indigenous communities and to all former course participants. For each course RITC receives up to 100 applications, and can only accommodate thirteen to fifteen individuals for the CEDO course, or four to five for the REDO course. In principle, RITC could accept more people for these courses, but at the moment funding will not allow it, as RITC pays for all expenses for each participant including travel, accommodation and material costs.

Lectures and interactive exercises are the most common methods used in the classroom. In Moscow, 'Study-visits' are also organized to appropriate NGO's, government departments and agencies, and donor organizations. For the REDO course, the 'illustrative' tour of Canadian indigenous communities offers a unique experience to learn first-hand from established organizations and businesses in a geographical setting similar to their Russian reality.

Methods used

Because of the ethnic diversity of the course participants, all the courses are conducted in Russian.

Language(s) of instruction

Structure of the Community Economic Development Officers' (CEDO) training course

Curriculum/Themes

- Introduction to Economics. The Market. Government regulation.
- Economics of traditional resource use and traditional economic activity.
- Communities of indigenous peoples: organizational principles, rights, responsibilities, and assets.
- Economic principles of organization activities.
- Labour relations. Special concerns regarding the conclusion of labour contracts. Occupational safety.
- Financial principles of organization activities.
- Special features of accounting and taxation for non-commercial organizations.
- Marketing and the marketing environment.

- Management: personnel and financial.
- Special aspects of the management of non-commercial organizations and small businesses.
- Basic principles of business planning.
- Non-commercial finances and fund-raising.
- Licensing and certification. Licensing of traditional product exports.

Structure of the Regional Economic Development Officers' (REDO) training course

- Status of indigenous peoples in Russia. Presentations (by the interns, RAIPON and RITC).
- Russian Federation: administrative divisions (federal *okrugs*, national republics, *krais* and *oblasts*, autonomous districts) and their relationships.
- International laws and standards protecting the rights of indigenous peoples. Federal legislation and approaches to problems relating to the vital activities of indigenous peoples and the economic activities of communities. Overview of regional legislation.
- Types of organizations and businesses of indigenous peoples established by federal law. Instructional visit to the Russian Federation State Duma.
- Natural resources and traditional resource use: reindeer herding, hunting, fishing, non-timber resources, crafts, and tourism. New approaches and opportunities.
- Organization: structure and functions. Management (including financial planning). Investments and the non-commercial sector.
- Preparation of business plans. Instructional visit to the Ministry of Economic Development and Trade. The federal programme of support for indigenous peoples through 2010.
- Fund-raising. Supervising work with donors and

other sources of funding. Internet resources. Various programmes to protect the rights of indigenous peoples.
- Instructional visits to donor Foundations, relevant Embassies, the World Bank office, the mission of the European Commission in Russia, and to the United Nations Development Programme (UNDP) office.

Joint programme:
Interns from regional administrations and interns from the course for regional co-ordinators

- Legal principles governing small business
- How to work with various levels of government
- Indigenous peoples and government: from paternalism to partnership
- Local development strategies
- Preparation of specific proposals (practical session).

Specialized educational modules are offered for the following sectors:

- Management
- Law
- Economics
- Accounting.

Sector modules are offered for the following fields:

- Tourism
- Reindeer herding, hunting and fur trading and related services
- Fishing and fishing services
- Logging and harvesting of wild plants and non-timber forest products
- Souvenir products

- Foreign economic activity
- Environmental activities
- Social services.

New training courses to be developed by RITC in 2003 and 2004, within the framework of a TACIS-funded project

- Legislation
- Psychology of Management
- Land and Natural Resources
- Principles of Co-Management
- Aboriginal Culture and Heritage
- Environmental Protection
- Principles of Sustainable Development and their Implementation in the Life of Northern Indigenous People.

In 2004 – 2005, these new courses will be conducted in different combinations at six seminars, each to be attended by ten to fifteen participants. Applications from potential trainees and selection procedures will follow the same principles already in place (open application process, selection with respect to balance of regions, ethnic groups, gender). For each course, relevant guidelines/manuals will be produced.

Teachers/Training   RITC invites experts to teach each of the course subjects. Indigenous teachers are given first priority, but at the moment it is difficult to find indigenous instructors with a strong economic background. This is important because the current focus of RITC is to offer training which will promote community and regional economic development. All specialists must have economic development in their background and must be experienced in working with indigenous communities.

Printed materials produced by RITC

- *Economic and Management Basics of an Organization* – a manual for indigenous communities of the North, Siberia and the Far East of the Russian Federation, by T. V. Bocharnikova, RITC trainer.
- Manual for working with donor organizations on projects related to indigenous peoples of the North of the Russian Federation.
- *Strengthening Indigenous Peoples' NGOs: List of Donor Agencies* (Year 2002 edition).
- Legal Handbook and Manual (recommendations) for traditional indigenous activities.
- Manuals for the training course (produced for each training course separately).

A *RITC Newsletter* had been published three to four times a year with a distribution list of approximately 300. Eight issues had been distributed by September 2003, when the *Newsletter* was transformed into a quarterly magazine entitled *Economics of Indigenous Peoples*.

Manuals will continue to be produced for the economic development courses offered by RITC in the future. It is expected that as RITC expands its training courses, materials will be developed for courses offered on cultural and social issues, environmental issues, legal issues, renewable and non-renewable resource issues, etc.

Apart from training, another activity of RITC is to financially support RAIPON's very important participation in the work of the Arctic Council (an international circumpolar forum made up of Ministerial representatives from the eight Arctic nations of Russia, the United States, Canada, Denmark, Iceland, Sweden, Norway and Finland).

Outcomes

In the first three years of the Project (with two years remaining):

- Forty-five indigenous people of 14 indigenous nationalities, representing 15 administrative regions and 37 communities, have been trained as community economic development officers.
- Nine regional economic development officers have been trained, and five continue their work in Khanty-Mansyisk Autonomous region, in the Republic of Sakha (Yakutia), in Anadyr' (Chukotka), in Krasnoyarsky Krai, and in the Taimyr.
- The regionalization of RITC began with the establishment of the Taimyr RITC branch office, which is supported by the Taimyr Government. The RITC staff have conducted their first seminar, and the Taimyr Branch has since carried out two additional training seminars for a total of seventy people.
- Establishment of a distribution list, which is used for disseminating information on upcoming courses, RITC activities, and relevant information relating to economic development, etc. The current distribution list includes over 500 individual contacts (the total number of indigenous applicants to the courses), 34 regional associations, and 272 indigenous communities, in 29 administrative regions of the Russian Federation.
- Over half of those trained in all RITC courses are women.
- A *Manual to Donor Agencies* with an interest in Northern, indigenous and environmental areas has been produced and is now being used, not only as a reference guide, but as a training tool in RITC courses.
- RAIPON's organizational capacity continues to be strengthened through the financial support provided to them by the Project for their participation on the Arctic Council.

- RITC has produced a number of training manuals (see above), which are used during training sessions.
- A database is being established on the indigenous communities of the Russian North, which because of its up-to-date and accurate community profiles could become a source of revenue generation for RITC.
- RITC, in September 2003, was successful in its first fund-raising application and has been awarded monies, over a two-year period, to develop an 'Educational System for Sustainable Development of Indigenous Peoples of the Russian North'.

Strengths

- The training programmes are designed to contribute to the maintenance of the indigenous culture and way of life while at the same time providing the skills and tools necessary to promote income generation and the self-sufficiency of the communities, in the context of a market economy.
- The courses are needed: there is an overwhelming demand for economics-related knowledge in all regions, and particularly in the indigenous communities. The number of applications for each course far exceeds current RITC capacity (physically and financially).
- RITC's good programmes and high-quality experts are very much appreciated by all trainees. This is reflected in the *Course Evaluations* that the participants of every training course are required to complete.
- Increasing credibility with the indigenous communities. All trainees applying for the course must submit, with their application, a *letter of recommendation* from their local indigenous community or

Lessons learnt: strengths and weaknesses

organization. This enhances the community/RITC relationship and promotes continuing community support for participants upon their return.

- Positive feedback by course participants, who say they are continuously using the knowledge and skills learned during their training, and that it helps them substantially in the development of their community-based businesses.
- Each course offered is gender-equal.
- Interest by some regions in establishing a branch office of RITC.
- Increasing demand for training to be taken to the regions, instead of bringing the participants to Moscow. RITC is currently negotiating with six regional authorities to provide courses locally, for which the regional administrations will pay all expenses.
- Increasing demand for RITC to expand the courses being offered to other subject areas of importance and interest to the indigenous peoples of the Russian North.

Weaknesses

- Courses are dependant on external funding. All training courses which have been offered by RITC thus far were paid for by INRIPP-II (international development project funded by the Canadian International Development Agency [CIDA]). RITC covers all travel and accommodation costs for all participants and trainers. The number of training courses per year, location of these courses, and the content of the courses will be expanded when RITC and/or the participants themselves are able to raise local and regional in-country financial support.
- As of Spring 2003, the concrete effects of the training courses on the communities were not known.

This is now being rectified with the strengthening of the Outreach Department. Recently RITC was able to intensify its post-course communication with the trainees to get assessments from all of them on how the training courses influenced their performance in economic development of their communities and businesses. All RITC staff now realize the value of such post-course follow-up and intend to devote more attention to maintaining contact with the participants. Trainees are now being encouraged to write their success stories for publication in the RITC quarterly magazine *Economics of Indigenous Peoples*.

- Restricted number of courses and experts involved. In the years 2000 – 2002, there were only two basic courses, each conducted by four to six key experts. The reason for this relates partly to funding, but also to the fact that there are still very few specialists in the country experienced in both economic development and indigenous issues. This challenge is well recognized by RITC, and development of new courses with the involvement of new experts is foreseen in the coming year.
- Losing trained Regional Economic Development Officers, which we acknowledge will be an on-going problem, as once people receive more training, their job opportunities expand.
- The regular shifting of the Russian federal government department responsible for indigenous affairs has frustrated the progress of RITC, because each time a new department is assigned the responsibility, the orientation process begins again.
- Lack of indigenous instructors.

Duration

The Russian Indigenous Training Centre's original project funding is for five years, from the summer of 2000 to the summer of 2005. It is intended that the Centre will become financially self-sufficient on a long-term basis and, hopefully, be in existence for many years after the original Project funding ends.

Funding/Budget

RITC is currently funded under the 'Aboriginal Component' of the *Institution-Building for Northern Russian Indigenous Peoples Project (INRIPP II)* and has a five-year budget of approximately Can$2 million. Funding is provided by the Canadian International Development Agency (CIDA).

Responsible organization(s)

The INRIPP II project was initiated by the Canadian office of the Inuit Circumpolar Conference (ICC, an international Inuit NGO), and, while CIDA funds the Project, ICC (Canada) is the executing agency in partnership with the Russian Association of Indigenous Peoples of the North (RAIPON), the Federal Canadian Department of Indian Affairs and Northern Development (DIAND), and the Federal Russian Ministry of Economic Development and Trade.

Contact

Director: Rodion Sulyandziga
Russian Indigenous Training Centre
Mailing address:
P.O. Box 110, Moscow, 119415
Russia
Phone: +7 (095) 945 66 82
Phone/fax: +7 (095) 255 5623
E-mail: ritc@mail.ru
Website: http://www.csipn.ru

NOTE

1. This case study is a joint contribution by Rodion Sulyandziga (RITC Director), Oleg Shakov (INRIPP II Project Manager), Dr Lena Lebedeva (RITC Outreach Coordinator) and Wendy Ellis (INRIPP II Canadian Facilitator).

UNITED STATES (ALASKA): ALASKA STANDARDS FOR CULTURALLY RESPONSIVE SCHOOLS AND THE ALASKA RURAL SYSTEMIC INITIATIVE [1]
AKRSI and ANKN

Reform Initiatives for schools and educators serving native students in Alaska at all grade levels

Type of programme and educational level

The state of Alaska (United States), with a focus on rural schools serving native communities and involving native and non-native as well as governmental and non-governmental institutions

Geographic and administrative aspects

Native students, educators, schools, communities and others

Indigenous target groups/Beneficiaries

This case study describes two interrelated initiatives promoting reforms in Alaska Native Education: the Alaska Rural Systemic Initiative (AKRSI) and the *Alaska Standards for Culturally Responsive Schools*.

Description of programme/institution

Summary

 The Alaska Rural Systemic Initiative started in 1995, based on an implementation plan for a five-year initiative that was developed by an Alaska Native/Rural Education Consortium, established by the Alaska Federation of Natives in co-operation with the University of Alaska Fairbanks. The underlying purpose of the AKRSI has been to implement a set of initiatives to document the indigenous knowledge systems of Alaska Native people and develop pedagogical practices and school curricula that appropriately incorporate indigenous knowledge and ways of knowing into the formal education system. The central focus of the AKRSI's reform strategy has been the promotion of interconnectivity and complementarity between these two functionally interdependent but historically disconnected and alienated knowledge systems (AKRSI, 2000, p. 2).

The curriculum and professional development initiatives of the AKRSI are coupled with the sponsorship of a series of regional Native Educator Associations and of the annual meetings of the statewide Native Educator's Conference, hosted by the Native Educator Associations. At the second Native Educators Conference held in Anchorage, in 1998, the Alaska Standards for Culturally Responsive Schools, developed by Alaska Native educators for schools and educators serving native students, were adopted. The Cultural Standards embody the reform strategy of the AKRSI. They were published by the Alaska Native Knowledge Network (ANKN) in 1998 and are now in use in schools throughout Alaska (AKRSI, 2001, p. 4).

These standards provide guidelines against which schools and communities can examine the extent to which they are attending the educational and cultural well-being of students. They include standards in five areas: for students, educators, curriculum, schools and communities.

Since 1998, these standards have been complemented by a set of further guidelines also adopted by the Assembly of Alaska Native Educators at the annual sessions of the Native Educators Conference and published by ANKN. These include:

- *Guidelines for Preparing Culturally Responsive Teachers for Alaska's Schools* (1999)
- *Guidelines for Respecting Cultural Knowledge* (2000)
- *Guidelines for Strengthening Indigenous Languages* (2001)

- *Guidelines for Nurturing Culturally Healthy Youth* (2001)
- *Guidelines for Culturally Responsive School Boards* (2002)
- *Guidelines on Cross-Cultural Orientation Programmes* (2003).

These complementary guidelines are addressed, among others, to native Elders, parents and communities, to schools, teachers, researchers, publishers and policy-makers with different focus and emphasis. However, they are all rooted in the belief that a form of education grounded in the heritage language and culture indigenous to a particular place is a fundamental prerequisite for the development of culturally healthy students and communities.

Approximately 40 per cent of the 553,600 people living in Alaska are spread out in 240 small, isolated communities ranging in size from 25 to 5,000, with the remaining 60 per cent concentrated in a handful of 'urban' centres, and with nearly 50 per cent of the total population living in Anchorage. Of the rural communities, over 200 are remote, predominantly native (Aleut, Eskimo and Indian) villages in which 70 per cent of the 86,300 Alaska Natives live. The vast majority of the native people in rural Alaska continue to rely on subsistence hunting and fishing, coupled with a slowly evolving cash-based economy, for a significant portion of their livelihood, since few permanent jobs exist in most communities. According to a 1990 survey, the percentage of people living in 'poverty' in rural communities in Alaska ranges from 15 per cent to 57 per cent, with the average income in the US$7,000 to US$15,000 range.

Background: legal-political, socio-economic, educational and linguistic situation

In the mid-1970s, the passage of the Alaska Native Claims Settlement Act by the US Congress in 1971, legal actions, the growing political power of Alaska Natives and the inadequacy of centralized education systems led to changes in the administration of rural schools which until then was in the hands of either the federal Bureau of Indian Affairs or the Alaska State-Operated School System. Twenty-one locally controlled regional school districts were established to take over the responsibility for providing education in rural communities and 126 village high schools were created to serve those rural communities where high school students had to leave home to attend boarding schools. This has provided rural communities with an opportunity to exercise a greater degree of political control over the educational systems operating in rural Alaska. However, it did not lead to any appreciable change in what is taught and how it is taught in those systems (ANKN webpage summarizing the AKRSI).

For several years, Alaska has been developing 'content standards' to define what students should know and be able to do as they go through school. In addition, 'performance standards' are being developed for teachers and administrators, and a set of 'quality school standards' have been put forward by the Alaska Department of Education to serve as a basis for accrediting schools in Alaska. As these state standards are written for general use throughout Alaska, they do not always address some of the special issues that are of critical importance to schools in rural Alaska, particularly those serving Alaska Native communities and students (ANKN, 1998, p. 2). Therefore, Alaska Native educators have developed the 'cultural standards' as complementary to the standards adopted by the State of Alaska.

Objectives and focus

The focus of the Alaska Rural Systemic Initiative is to provide an opportunity for the people of Alaska, particularly Alaska Natives, to formulate a renewed educational agenda regarding the structure, content and processes that are needed to increase the involvement of Alaska Native people in the application of native and non-native scientific knowledge to the solution of human problems in an Arctic environment. This centres on two key elements of change around which the AKRSI educational reform strategy has been constructed:

1. The Alaska Native professional educators working in the formal education system coupled with the native Elders who are the culture-bearers for the indigenous knowledge system.
2. The rural teachers/schools implementing math/science performance standards and assessments (AKRSI, 2000, p. 2).

The overall project is organized into five major initiatives which have been implemented during Phase I of the AKRSI (1995–2000), and are continued during Phase II (2000–05), with distinct emphasis on a rotating basis in the following regions: Yup'ik, Southeast, Aleut/Alutiq, Athabascan, and Inupiaq Region. This is illustrated in the following table (adapted from the AKRSI, 2001, p. 2):

Regional Initiative	Initiative Emphasis
Native Ways of Knowing and Teaching	Parent Involvement
Culturally Aligned Curriculum	Cultural Standards
Indigenous Science Knowledge	Cultural Atlas
Elders and Cultural Camps	Academy of Elders
Village Science Applications/Careers	ANSES Camps/Fairs

The objective of the cultural standards, adopted during Phase I of the AKRSI, is to provide a way for schools, educators and communities to examine what they are doing to attend the cultural well-being of the young people they are responsible for educating through to adulthood. Even though this focuses on rural schools serving native communities, many of the standards are applicable to all students and communities because curricular attention is focused on in-depth study of the surrounding physical and cultural environment in which the school is situated, while recognizing the unique contribution that indigenous people can make to such study as long-term inhabitants who have accumulated extensive specialized knowledge related to that environment (ANKN, 1998, pp. 2–3).

Participation

The Alaska Rural Systemic Initiative is currently concentrating its initiatives on twenty rural school districts, containing 176 schools and approximately 90 per cent of the Alaska Native student population in rural Alaska. These have historically produced the lowest achievement scores in the state, and native people have been the most under-represented group in all aspects of math and science education and practice in Alaska. Five of these rural districts serve as the AKRSI 'focal districts' and contain a total of 8,351 students in 61 schools served by 791 certificated staff. However, other rural school districts and students throughout the state also participate in the AKRSI-sponsored activities – such as professional development workshops, native science fairs and science camps – and are impacted by changes in state policies and the utilization of culturally-aligned curriculum resources generated by the AKRSI (AKRSI, 2001, p. 3).

Through the Alaska Native/Rural Education Consortium, representatives from the rural school districts, State Department of Education, university campuses, native organizations, Elders, and other related agencies and professional organizations are brought together yearly to be briefed on the status of the AKRSI initiatives, to report on their own work related to those initiatives, and to co-ordinate their efforts in ways that will maximize the impact. Subcontracts are established with these partners, capitalizing on their role and strength, and results and experiences are shared and built upon as each initiative shifts from on region to the next on a rotating basis. Parents and Elders are involved in all aspects of the AKRSI implementation (AKRSI, 2001, pp. 9–10).

The cultural standards and subsequent guidelines have been developed through a series of regional and state-wide meetings associated with and sponsored by the Alaska Rural Systemic Initiative and involving many Native Educator Associations (see list at end of chapter). The standards and guidelines have been adopted by the Assembly of Alaska Native Educators.

With regard to participation, the standards and guidelines themselves emphasize the importance of extensive community and parental interaction and involvement in their children's education, both in and out of school. Elders, parents and local leaders should be involved in all aspects of instructional planning and the design and implementation of programmes and curricula. Culturally responsive schools foster extensive ongoing participation, communication and interaction between school and community personnel and provide regular opportunities for local and regional board deliberations and decision-making on policy, programme and person- nel issues related to the school (ANKN, 1998, p. 20).

Furthermore, educational material, in particular material in the local language and including cultural knowledge, needs to be developed, produced and reviewed by or with the participation of culturally knowledgeable community members. In particular, Eld- ers are accorded a central role as the primary source of knowledge throughout the standards and guidelines. Their cultural and professional expertise is essential and should be used in an appropriate way.

The emphasis is on fostering a strong connection between what students experience in school and their lives out of school by providing opportunities for students to engage in in-depth experiential learning in real world contexts (ANKN, 1998, p. 3). **Methods used**

Culturally responsive education is directed toward cul- turally knowledgeable students who are well grounded in the cultural heritage and traditions of their community and are able to understand how their local situation and knowledge relates to the wider situation around them and other knowledge systems and cultural beliefs. This involves:

- multiple avenues for the incorporation of locally recognized expertise in all actions related to the use and interpretation of local cultural knowledge and practices as the basis for learning about the larger world
- reinforcing the positive parenting and child-rearing practices from the community in all aspects of teaching and engaging in extended experiences that involve the development of observation and listening skills associated with the traditional learning ways of native people
- cultural and language immersion programmes and the organization and implementation of extended camps and other seasonal everyday-life experiences in order to ground student learning naturally in the surrounding environment (ANKN, 1999, pp. 6–7).

The initiatives implemented and promoted by the AKRSI include regional and statewide workshops and conferences, teacher development, regional Scientist-in-Residence programmes, native science and cultural camps for teachers, student projects involving data collection and analysis in their local environment, and collaborative research initiatives, as ways to promote educational reform at all levels and include the perspectives of the various educational actors involved.

An important element of building upon the traditional learning styles of indigenous peoples is the creation and maintenance of multiple avenues for Elders to interact formally and informally with students at all times. This includes opportunities for students to engage in the documenting of Elders' cultural knowledge on a regular basis, thereby contributing to the maintenance and transmission of cultural knowledge. The implementation of Elders-in-Residence programmes in schools and classrooms, which means involving Elders in teaching and curriculum development in a formal educational setting, represents a useful and much supported avenue in this regard (ANKN, 2000, pp. 11, 26).

The AKRSI, based on a successful initiative during Phase I, sponsors a process called 'Academy of Elders'.

An Academy is made up of native teachers, Elders and practicing scientists and science teachers, all of whom gather for a week or more at a camp or village site where the Elders and scientists pass on their knowledge in reference to some aspect of the local environment to the teachers. The teachers are then responsible for developing curricular applications for what they have learned, checking with the Elders and scientists for its accuracy, and then pilot testing it in the classroom to determine how effective it is with students. These refined curriculum units are then compiled and put onto the AKRSI website and into publication form for distribution to other teachers and schools (AKRSI, 2001, p. 3).

The *Handbook for Culturally Responsive Science Curriculum* provides further information on how to approach and involve Elders as teachers. It also highlights how traditional teaching and learning can be combined with strategies for teaching inquiry-based science. Some compatible strategies include:

- community involvement and co-operative groups
- multiple teachers as facilitators of learning
- investigate fundamental science questions related to life, seasons and environment
- investigate questions from multiple perspectives and disciplines
- learn by active and extended inquiry

- use of multiple sources of expert knowledge including cultural experts
- diverse representations and communication of student ideas and work to classmates and community (Stephens, p. 28).

Curriculum/Themes

'By shifting the focus in the curriculum from teaching/learning *about* cultural heritage as another subject to teaching/learning *through* the local culture as a foundation for all education, it is intended that all forms of knowledge, ways of knowing and world views be recognized as equally valid, adaptable and complementary to one another in mutually beneficial ways' (ANKN, 1998, p. 3).

In this respect, the incorporation of the Alaska Standards for Culturally Responsive Schools in all aspects of the school curriculum and the demonstration of their applicability in providing multiple avenues to meet the State Content Standards is central. Culturally responsive curricula:

- reinforce the integrity of the cultural knowledge that students bring with them
- recognize cultural knowledge as part of a living and constantly adapting system that is grounded in the past, but continues to grow through the present and into the future
- recognize cultural knowledge as a foundation for the rest of the curriculum and provide opportunities for students to study all subjects starting from a base in the local knowledge systems
- foster a complementary relationship across knowledge derived from diverse knowledge systems
- situate local knowledge and actions in a global context: 'think globally, act locally'
- unfold in a physical environment that is inviting and readily accessible for local people to enter and utilize (ANKN, 1998, pp. 13 19).

The Alaska Standards for Culturally Responsive Schools provide teachers and other educational actors with explicit guidelines for the implementation of a culturally aligned, standards-based curriculum. The AKRSI has created a curriculum clearinghouse to identify, review and catalogue appropriate national and Alaska-based curriculum resources suitable for rural/native settings, and to make them available throughout the state via the AKRSI website. This has been expanded in Phase II with a CD-ROM collection of the best materials in various thematic areas most relevant to schools in rural Alaska.

As a means of organizing all the curricular and cultural resources that are emerging from the schools as a result of the various initiatives, the AKRSI has developed the 'Spiral Pathway for Integrating Rural Learning' (SPIRAL). Resources for various themes and grade levels, including hands-on examples and experiences of how to put the cultural standards into practice in the development of curricula, are being compiled and made available on-line through the SPIRAL on the ANKN website.

SPIRAL is structured around twelve themes: Family, Language/Communication, Cultural Expression, Tribe/Community, Health/Wellness, Living in Place, Outdoor Survival, Subsistence, ANCSA (Alaska Native Land Claims Settlement Act), Applied Technology, Energy/Ecology, and Exploring Horizons (AKRSI, 2001, pp. 7, 9).

One such resource is the Handbook for Culturally Responsive Science Curriculum, which provides further insight, practical information, and examples of how to incorporate traditional knowledge in science curricula and integrate it with Western science, how to relate topics to the cultural standards, as well as examples of culturally appropriate strategies for instruction and assessment. The following is an example for the development of a culturally relevant science unit, meeting and integrating the cultural standards with Alaska State science and math standards:

SNOWSHOES

Grade Level: 5 – 6
Region: Athabascan
Context: winter for two weeks or potentially more

Cultural Standards
A4 – Practice their traditional responsibilities to the surrounding environment
D1 – Acquire in-depth cultural knowledge through active participation and meaningful interaction with Elders

Skills and Knowledge
Know which types of snowshoes are appropriate for which conditions
Demonstrate traditional weaving techniques and integrate with tessellation
Show how to properly take care of snowshoes
develop respect for Elders and others who have traditional knowledge and skills

Science Standards
D1 – Apply scientific knowledge and skills to understand issues and everyday events

Skills and Knowledge
Apply understanding of the concept of weight distribution over a specific area to the construction of snowshoes, and
Identify different types of snowshoes and describe the importance of the various shapes in forested or open areas

Math Standards
A2 – Select and use appropriate systems, units, and tools of measurement, including estimation

A4 – Represent, analyse, and use mathematical patterns, relations and functions using methods such as tables, equations, and graphs

Skills and Knowledge
Compare and contrast Western means of measuring (rulers) with native use of anatomical measures
Conduct a survey of how many snowshoe types, sizes, who owns them, etc., in their community and graphically display the results (Stephens, p. 20)

The cultural standards and in particular the *Guidelines for Strengthening Indigenous Languages* hope to promote the daily use of indigenous languages throughout Alaska and encourage the support of educational institutions in order to perpetuate these languages. Schools serve a supportive role by providing appropriate language immersion programmes that strengthen the language used in the community[2] (ANKN, 2001a, p. 2). The standards and guidelines emphasize the utilization of the local language as a base from which to learn the deeper meanings of the local cultural knowledge, values, beliefs and practices. To keep a language going, it must be used as much as possible in everyday activities, at home and in the community.

    Native Elders, as the essential resources through whom the heritage language of a community and the meaning it is intended to convey can be learned, and parents, as the first teachers of their children, play an important role and need to assume their responsibilities in this regard. It is important that parents participate in all aspects of a child's upbringing, including joint learning of the heritage language (if the child is not already a fluent speaker) as a way of demonstrating the importance of the effort (ANKN, 2001a, pp. 4, 6). This language policy promoted by the guidelines is also supported and implemented by the AKRSI.

Language of instruction

To sum up, the standards and guidelines support/advocate initial instruction in the local/heritage language to learn about the local culture and knowledge, and that learning of and through a second language, and about other cultures and knowledge, happens on the basis of knowledge and literacy in the local language. Instruction in the local/heritage language should be offered through to the highest grade-level, including the provision of heritage language courses for students in every high school in Alaska, especially those with native students enrolled, and of courses that acquaint all students with the heritage language of the local community.

Teachers

Many rural schools in Alaska face a high turnover rate for teachers and are affected by a growing teacher shortage in general. Only 6 per cent of the certified personnel employed in the twenty rural districts involved with the AKRSI initiatives are Alaska Native teachers. Therefore, the emphasis of the AKRSI has been on those changes that can bring about a higher degree of stability and continuity in the professional personnel in those schools, and particularly on the preparation of greater numbers of well-qualified Alaska Native teachers and administrators. This means focusing leadership development on those teachers for whom the community/region/state is their home.

The AKRSI started a Teacher Leadership Development Project in October 2001 which focuses on capacity-building, curriculum workshops, conferences for math/science educators, native science and cultural camps and the 'Academy of Elders' process, mentioned before, in partnership with the regional and statewide Native Educator Associations that have emerged in response to the AKRSI initiatives over the past years (AKRSI, 2001, pp. 3–5).

The Project represents an effective example in terms of meeting the following standard of culturally responsive schools:

- A culturally responsive school has a high level of involvement of professional staff who are of the same cultural background as the students with whom they are working and encourages and supports the professional development of local personnel to assume teaching and administrative roles in the school (ANKN, 1998, p. 19).

The AKRSI's initiatives with regard to curriculum and professional development are connected to the development of the Alaska Standards for Culturally Responsive Schools and the *Guidelines for the Preparation of Culturally Responsive Teachers* which are being incorporated in the AKRSI's initiatives for teacher development. According to the Alaska Standards for Culturally Responsive Schools, culturally responsive educators:

- incorporate local ways of knowing and teaching in their work
- use the local environment and community resources on a regular basis to link what they are teaching to the everyday lives of the students
- participate in community events and activities in an appropriate and supportive way
- work closely with parents to achieve a high level of complementary educational expectations between home and school
- recognize the full educational potential of each student and provide challenges necessary for them to achieve that potential (ANKN, 1998, pp. 9–12).

The Guidelines for Preparing Culturally Responsive Teachers for Alaska's Schools were adopted in 1999 to complement these standards. They provide assistance in the preparation and training of teachers – who will be expected to teach students of diverse backgrounds in a culturally responsive way – and in determining the enhanced knowledge and skills that culturally responsive teachers need above and beyond the performance indicators stipulated by the state Alaska Teacher Standards (ANKN, 1999, p. 2).

Materials and activities   Materials and activities used and applied in culturally responsive education reflect a complementary relationship of diverse knowledge systems. This includes drawing parallels between knowledge derived from oral tradition and that derived from books, as well as the construction of new knowledge in the learning-teaching process (ANKN, 1998, p. 15).

It further includes materials based on natural and community resources and experiential learning activities in the surrounding environment as means of acquiring local cultural knowledge and as a basis for learning the conventional curriculum content as outlined in state standards.

The Alaska Standards for Culturally Responsive Schools point to the need for:

- opportunities for regular engagement of students in the documenting of Elders' cultural knowledge through which appropriate print and multimedia materials that share this knowledge with others can be produced
- utilizing local expertise, including that of students, in providing culturally appropriate materials, such as displays of arts, crafts and other forms of decoration and space design in schools
- utilizing technology as a tool to enhance educational opportunities and to facilitate appropriate documentation and communication of local cultural knowledge while honoring cultural and intellectual property rights
- sponsoring on-going activities and events in the school and community that celebrate and provide opportunities for students to put into practice and display their knowledge of local cultural traditions. (ANKN, 1998, pp. 17, 20).

As regards teaching of math and science, for example, it is essential to develop curriculum resource materials that guide teachers in the use of local environment and cultural resources in order to promote hands-on, inquiry-based instruction. In this regard, various forms of science/culture camps are an important vehicle, as examples from schools participating in the AKRSI illustrate (AKRSI, 2001, p. 7).

As for instruction in the local language, the use of locally produced resource materials (e.g. reports, videos, maps, books, tribal documents) in the local language, in all subject areas – in close collaboration with local agencies, and encouraging and supporting native authors – can enrich the curriculum beyond the scope of commercially produced texts (ANKN, 2001a, p. 16). When producing, using and incorporating local cultural knowledge in education material, it should be ensured that all cultural content has been acquired under informed consent and has been reviewed and approved for accuracy and appropriateness by knowledgeable local people who are representative of the culture in question. When documenting oral history, the power of the written word – and the implications of putting oral tradition, with all its non-verbal connotations, down on paper – should be considered, always striving to convey the original meaning and context as much as possible (ANKN, 2000, pp. 6–7).

Outcomes

The AKRSI-sponsored Alaska Standards for Culturally Responsive Schools have been adopted by the State Board of Education and have recently been incorporated in the state Curriculum Frameworks document. They are in use in schools throughout the state, and their positive reception is evinced by the steadily growing requests for materials listed in the ANKN database. The ready availability of these resources has given school districts the impetus to renew their curricula so as to integrate the model based on the cultural standards that have been promoted by the AKRSI (AKRSI, 2001, pp. 7, 9).

Some of the effects and changes generated through the AKRSI's initiatives, the cultural standards and complementary guidelines include:

- The reallocation of both state and federal funds to support initiatives such as science camps, documentation of cultural resources by students, student projects involving data collection and analysis in their local environment, increasing involvement of Elders as knowledge resources, use of technology to record and analyse data, etc.
- The development of the Alaska Quality Schools Initiative, through which policy changes relating to standards-based curriculum and assessment are being implemented, to ensure that appropriate consideration is given to Alaska Native issues in the process (AKRSI, 2001, p. 5)
- The sponsorship of several regional science camps focusing on helping students (and teachers) recognize the many facets of science that are practiced in the everyday activities of the people in their communities, including the scientific knowledge imbedded in many of the traditional activities of the local native people (AKRSI, 2000, p. 8)
- The consistent improvement of students' academic performance in the AKRSI partner schools exemplifies the positive impact of the use of the Alaska Standards for Culturally Responsive Schools in terms of increasing the connections between what students experience in school and what they experience outside of school (AKRSI, 2001, p. 14).

Lessons learnt: strengths and weaknesses

The educational reform strategy chosen by the AKRSI continues to produce:

- an increase in student achievement scores
- a decrease in the dropout rate

- an increase in the number of rural students attending college
- an increase in the number of native students choosing to pursue studies in fields of science, math and engineering, and
- an increased interest and involvement of native people in education in rural communities throughout Alaska (AKRSI, 2001, p. 14).

The AKRSI started in 1995 and has gone into its second phase (2000 2005).

Duration

Funding for the AKRSI, the workshops, and the meetings of the Native Educators Conference is provided by the National Science Foundation and the Annenberg Rural Challenge (now The Rural School and Community Trust Fund), supplemented by additional funding from other sources for specific AKRSI initiatives.

Funding/Budget

The Alaska Rural Systemic Initiative, Alaska Native Knowledge Network, University of Alaska Fairbanks, and the following Native Educator Associations and institutions which endorsed the Alaska Standards for Culturally Responsive Schools:

Responsible institutions and organization

Alaska Federation of Natives, Alaska Rural Challenge, Ciulistet Research Association, Association of Interior Native Educators, Southeast Native Educators Association, North Slope Inupiaq Educators Association, Association of Native Educators of the Lower Kuskokwim, Association of Northwest Native Educators, Alaska Native Education Student Association, Alutiiq Native Educator Association, Unangan Educator Association, Alaska Native Education Council, Alaska Native Teachers for Excellence/Anchorage, Consortium for Alaska Native Higher Education, Alaska First Nations Research Network, Center For Cross-Cultural Studies, Alaska State Board of Education.

Contact   Alaska Native Knowledge Network
               University of Alaska Fairbanks
               P.O. Box 756730
               Fairbanks
               AK 99775-6730
               Tel: + 1 (907) 474-5897
               Website: http://www.ankn.uaf.edu

NOTES

1. The information in this case study largely represents a summary of the main issues addressed in the cultural standards and subsequent guidelines and of the initiatives of the Alaska Rural Systemic Initiative (AKRSI). We acknowledge the support of Sean Topkok from ANKN and Ray Barnhardt of the AKRSI who provided us with information and reviewed the first draft of the case study. The sources and more detailed information and examples can be found on the ANKN website at http://www.ankn.uaf.edu:

   ANKN, 1998: *Alaska Standards for Culturally Responsive Schools*
   ANKN, 1999: *Guidelines Preparing Culturally Responsive Teachers for Alaska's Schools*
   ANKN, 2000: *Guidelines for Respecting Cultural Knowledge*
   ANKN, 2001: *Guidelines for Strengthening Indigenous Languages*
   ANKN, 2001: *Guidelines for Nurturing Culturally Healthy Youth*
   ANKN, 2002: *Guidelines for Culturally Responsive School Boards*
   ANKN, 2003: *Guidelines for Cross-Cultural Orientation Programs*
   ANKN, Themes of the Spiral Curriculum Chart at http://www.ankn.uaf.edu/spiral.html
   ANKN webpage for a summary of the AKRSI http://www.ankn.uaf.edu/akrsi
   Stephens, Sidney, 2000: *Handbook for Culturally Responsive Science Curriculum*
   AKRSI, 2000: AKRSI Final Report: Phase I (1995–2000)
   AKRSI, 2001: AKRSI Annual Report: Phase II, Year One. Retrieved from http://www.ankn.uaf.edu/AKRSIYearSix.pdf

UNITED STATES (ARIZONA): LEUPP NAVAJO IMMERSION PROJECT

Michael Fillerup

Formal bilingual programme for grades K-6 in Public School

Type of programme and educational level

Leupp Public School in the Navajo Nation, Arizona, United States; one of 20 schools in the Flagstaff Unified School District

Geographical and administrative level

A total of 230 students, of whom 99 per cent are Diné (Navajo)

Indigenous target group

Description of programme

Summary

This school-wide project is designed to help students become proficient speakers, readers, and writers of Navajo, while enhancing their English language skills and preparing them to meet state academic standards. The programme combines Navajo immersion with ESL (English as a Second Language) inclusion, literacy initiatives, sheltered English/Navajo, parental involvement, and take-home technology. Academic content and state standards are initially presented from a Navajo perspective via four global themes with a unifying concept of *hózhó*, or 'peace, beauty and harmony'.

**Background:
legal-political,
socio-economic,
educational and
linguistic situation**

Of the twenty schools in the Flagstaff Unified School District (Flagstaff, AZ), Leupp is the only school in the district that is located on the Navajo Indian Reservation. It has the highest percentage of low-income students (98 per cent), the highest poverty rate (58 per cent), and the highest percentage of limited-English-proficient students (43 per cent). For years, it was also the poorest performing school in the district academically. Navajo language proficiency tests in the autumn of 1996 revealed that only 7 per cent of the students could speak Navajo fluently, while 11 per cent had limited proficiency, and 82 per cent had no proficiency.

Objectives and focus

- *Bilingualism*: Students will acquire the ability to speak, read, write, and communicate effectively in different social and cultural contexts in Navajo and in English.
- *Academic Achievement*: Students will meet the district and state standards in all academic subjects.
- *Cultural Enrichment*: Students will gain an in-depth understanding of the Navajo culture and its philosophical, historical, social, intellectual, and spiritual relationship to the social and academic mainstream.

Participation

We started with a survey of parents and community members to determine two things: (1) Do the parents and community of Leupp want a Navajo/English bilingual programme? (2) Will the parents and community support a bilingual programme if it is offered? We know that if the parents do not back the programme, or simply do not care, our efforts will be fruitless. Over 95 per cent of the parents 'greatly favour' a bilingual programme. Navajo parents actively participate on the school's site council, a decision-making body, as well as the school's Parent Advisory Committee. Local Elders frequently visit the school to conduct workshops on Navajo language and culture, tell stories in classrooms, perform traditional sweat ceremonies, and assist with other activities.

The heart of The Leupp Bilingual Education Project is to provide all Leupp students with an education that incorporates Navajo culture in all subject areas and is delivered largely via the Navajo language. However, there are other key components that supplement the Navajo language initiative, including:

Methods used

- *Take-home technology*
  Many students live in remote areas without electricity or running water, let alone home computers. Grant monies are used to purchase battery-powered laptop computers. These are checked out to students and parents who use the computers to complete specific classroom assignments at home.
- *Gifted services*
  A gifted resource teacher was hired to implement alternative measures to identify more gifted students, provide training to classroom teachers on how to incorporate critical thinking activities into the regular classroom curriculum, and provide supplementary services to gifted students.
- *Sheltered instruction*
  All classroom teachers are trained in the use of sheltered instructional strategies (i.e. extensive use of visuals, peer tutoring, co-operative learning, whole language instruction, thematic units, project-centred field-based activities, and so forth). Teachers write up an individualized Language Acquisition Plan, documenting how each child's academic, linguistic, social, and cultural needs will be met.
- *Family literacy and parent involvement*
  Leupp offers an Adult Education and Family Literacy Programme in which parents can earn a General Education Diploma (GED), improve

literacy skills, and learn basic math and other subjects. Beginning Navajo and Navajo literacy classes are offered free of charge.

- *Leupp/Sinagua High School Transition Program*
  A home/school co-ordinator is stationed at Sinagua High School to develop a programme to help Leupp students make the cultural, academic, and linguistic leap from an all-Indian K-8 reservation school (Leupp) to a predominately white high school in the city.
- *Intensified summer instruction*
  Federal government funds are used to extend learning opportunities by providing five weeks of summer school instruction to Leupp students. High school students from the Leupp community take classes for high school credit at no charge.

In addition to these components, the following initiatives are implemented to improve student literacy at Leupp:

- Sustained Silent Reading (SSR)
  All students and staff read silently for the first fifteen minutes of each school day.
- 'Read across the Rez' programme
  Students and classrooms are rewarded for the number of books read at home.
- Books in the homeThis initiative aims at placing ten additional books in the home of each Leupp student each year.
- Expanded library hours
  Leupp is pursuing an agreement with Coconino County to expand the collections and hours of the school library to serve Leupp and the surrounding community.

Languages of Instruction

In the fall of 1997, a committee consisting of Leupp faculty, staff, parents, and community members was formed to review and develop a blueprint for the Navajo language programme. Most committee members agreed that it would be best to teach students *in* the Navajo language rather than *about* the language. However, the amount of time that should be devoted to instruction via Navajo elicited a lengthy and lively discussion. In the end, the committee arrived at a compromise: Leupp students would be taught subject matter through the use of the Navajo language for at least half of the school day.

Because a major goal of the project is for all students to become proficient speakers, readers, and writers of Navajo and English, Language Arts are taught in both languages. Other subjects are taught in either English, Navajo, or both. For instance, social studies and science are more easily taught in Navajo than are technology or mathematics, which require contemporary terminology.

In kindergarten, about 90 per cent of the instruction is in Navajo. In first grade, the amount of Navajo and English instruction is equally divided. Our goal is to maintain that 50/50 balance in each subsequent grade. However, Navajo is currently being taught for only about an hour a day in Second, Third, and Fourth Grades, mainly for two reasons:

1. As the immersion programme expanded to higher grades, the classroom teachers were not Navajo speakers. Navajo instruction was delivered by a teaching assistant, which had the effect of placing Navajo in a subordinate role.
2. The emphasis in the state of Arizona, and in the United States generally, towards raising scores on standardized tests (which are written in English).

So, currently, the programme provides introductory immersion (in grade K-1), with Navajo enrichment in Grades 2 and above.

The Navajo Immersion Curriculum is Navajo-specific, meaning that subject matter is taught initially from a Navajo perspective. Students in Navajo Immersion

Curriculum/Themes

Programme are taught traditional Navajo forms of respect, including how to enter a hogan and how to greet people in the Navajo way. Building upon this foundation knowledge, mainstream culture is later taught within a broader context.

In the unit on plants (*Nanise'*), students learn about the importance of corn to the Navajo, as well as traditional uses of plants (i.e. for food, dyes, the arts, tools, medicine, and ceremonies). Students participate in the traditional practice of running to the East to greet the rising sun as part of the unit on exercise (*Naa' azdilts ood*). The unit on astronomy introduces students to Navajo constellations and Navajo beliefs about the heavens, as well as the Western view of astronomy.

Central to the Navajo culture is the concept of *hózhó*, or maintaining a life of 'peace, beauty and harmony'. Likewise, *hózhó* is the unifying theme of the Navajo Immersion Curriculum. All objectives and activities are designed to help students develop themselves intellectually, physically, spiritually, and socially, so they may 'walk in Beauty'. The curriculum is organized by fours, the sacred Navajo number.

Subject matter is presented holistically through four global themes, each representing one of the Four Sacred Mountains of the Navajo and its corresponding cardinal direction: Health: East (Mt. Blanca); Living Things: South (Mt. Taylor); Family & Community: West (San Francisco Peaks); Earth and Sky: North (Hesperus Peak). Each global theme is designed to be presented over a period of about nine weeks.

Four thematic units have been developed for each global theme. Each thematic unit includes a goal, objectives, key vocabulary and suggested activities. Objectives are correlated with the Arizona State Standards, and suggested activities are cross-referenced with the unit objectives.

The following is a sample thematic unit from the global theme *Family and Community*:

- Global theme: *Family and Community*: To develop an awareness of self and to perpetuate the Navajo language, culture and traditions relative to family, friends and community
- Thematic unit: Self (*Shí*)
- Thematic goal: To develop an awareness of self
- Objectives: The students will:

    1. demonstrate respect for themselves, class-mates, and others
    2. identify who they are by their two clan affiliations (maternal and paternal)
    3. identify Diné cultural values
    4. identify the parts of a cradle-board and explain its purpose
    5. identify the five senses
    6. identify the location of their home.

Suggested Activities (correlated with objectives):

- Perform student duties (1, 3)
- Make clan charts; introduce yourself (1, 2, 3, 6)
- Make a family tree with pictures (2)
- Make a model cradle-board (3, 4)
- Draw a self-portrait and label body parts (1, 5)
- Sing 'Shí Naashá' (1, 3)
- Make 'Me' books (1, 2, 3, 5, 6)
- Discuss and graph likes and dislikes (1, 5).

Subject matter is taught in an integrated manner. For example, the following Suggested Activity – *Visit local hogans; keep a sketchbook of types* – integrates four subject areas:

1. State Language Arts Standard 2: Communicate by drawing, telling, or writing.
2. District Social Studies Standard 10: Identify home, local neighbourhood, and school.

3.   State Math Standard 2: Collect, organize, and describe simple data.
4.   State Visual Arts Standard 1: Students know and apply the arts disciplines, techniques, and processes to communicate in original or interpretive work.

Teachers

Federal government monies are used to pay the tuition for teachers and staff to take college coursework towards state ESL or bilingual certification. In Leupp, we have six bilingual instructional aides and three certified Navajo-speaking teachers, one at kindergarten, one at first grade, and one at second grade. However, the long-term goal is to employ more Navajo-speaking teachers to be able to ensure immersion in Navajo through to higher grades.

Teachers and staff have completed a total of 518 credit hours of college coursework, or an average of 173 credit hours per year. The project provides extensive staff development opportunities, including tuition and books for college coursework, cultural workshops, and conferences. For example, during the first year of the project, all teachers and staff at Leupp (sixty-two total), thirteen from Sinagua High, five district-level administrators, and one school board member participate in Hooghan University, a series of workshops designed to sensitize individuals about Navajo culture.

Materials and activities

In the fall of 1999, a proposal to create a Navajo Cultural Center to be constructed on the grounds of Leupp Public School was presented. The Cultural Center will serve four functions:

•   Student Learning Center and Learning Lab
•   Community Learning Center
•   Global Resource Center
•   Cultural Arts Center

The Cultural Center will include a 600 square foot hogan, shade houses, a male sweat lodge, a female sweat lodge, a garden, and a sheep corral, and will facilitate a variety of activities, such as:

- Navajo language and culture classes
- Cultural and Historical Museum (of Leupp and the Navajo Reservation) designed, developed, and operated by Leupp students
- Community meetings and workshops
- Integrated thematic/academic projects
- Showcase for student academic work, arts, crafts, etc.
- Storytelling
- Traditional dances
- Tours provided by Leupp students
- Performances for students from other schools/ districts.

What we are striving for is a different way of teaching: a marriage between the traditional Navajo culture and contemporary knowledge and practices. This union is exemplified in our Cultural CD-ROM Project, where Leupp students interview Navajo Elders about their personal stories, videotape traditional weavers and artisans at work, and document various cultural traditions. This information is presented on the CD-ROM in Navajo with a voice-over in English. Using modern technology, Navajo students can work collaboratively with their elders to preserve their history, language, and culture.

Outcomes

Last spring (2001), the original cohort class took the Stanford (SAT) 9 test for the first time, as second graders. Twenty-three students were administered the test, including seventeen limited-English-proficient (LEP) and six non-LEP students. Although the sample size was small, the results were more than encouraging:

LEP students in the Navajo Immersion (NI) programme outperformed the average non-LEP student in the district by.4 Normal Curve Equivalent units (NCEs) in Reading and 7.8 NCEs in Math, while scoring within 6.3 NCEs in Language.

Second-grade students in the NI cohort also outperformed the previous year's (1999 – 2000) 'mostly English' second graders at Leupp in all three subtests.

Non-LEP second graders who had received almost all of their instruction in English averaged 54.0 NCEs in Reading, 62.0 NCEs in Math, and 44.0 NCEs in Language, while LEP students in the 'mostly English' programme averaged 23.3, 33.8, and 15.4 NCEs in Reading, Math, and Language, respectively. Non-LEP students in the NI programme outperformed their 'mostly English' non-LEP predecessors by 18, 9, and 8 NCEs, and LEP students in the NI programme outperformed the 'mostly English' LEP second graders by a staggering 33.1, 32.9, and 29.4 NCEs in Reading, Math, and Language, respectively.

While one SAT 9 test does not make or break a programme, this data should help to dispel any concerns about indigenous language immersion programmes having a detrimental effect on the English language development of native students, whether LEP or non-LEP. In fact, all of our data thus far indicates that the NI programme *accelerates* English language proficiency and academic achievement.

Finally, collaborative efforts have enabled the Leupp staff and community to incorporate Navajo culture throughout the school. Specifically, sweat lodges were built for traditional sweat ceremonies; a shade house was constructed by students as part of a thematic unit and is used for traditional school and community gatherings. In January 2002, a hogan, the traditional Navajo home, was formally dedicated on-site to serve as a school cultural centre and meeting place.

Lack of Certified Navajo Teachers

Lessons learnt: strengths and weaknesses

In the past, the bilingual aides provided Navajo language instruction for part of the day as an enrichment activity. However, this sent the wrong message to the students, in other words, that Navajo is a subordinate language, an add-on if we have time for it. Consequently, we are committed to having certified Navajo teachers in each immersion classroom working collaboratively with the Navajo-speaking aides. In the interim, the shortage of Navajo teachers can be addressed by creative scheduling, such as multi-age classroom teams – taught by a Navajo- and a non-Navajo-speaking teacher, the former providing the Navajo instruction, the latter the instruction in English.

Lack of Navajo-Language Materials

The lack of native-language content materials, especially in the upper grades, remains a serious problem. The Navajo-language materials market is too small to attract major commercial publishers, so we, like other Navajo programmes on the reservation, continue to laboriously develop our own materials while relying on the efforts of the Navajo Curriculum Centres that survived the funding cuts in the eighties.

Lack of Navajo Testing Materials

Instruments to assess language and content knowledge via Navajo are as scarce as Navajo-language materials. We develop, borrow, and adapt as we go. Testing materials are neither normed nor standardized, and thus there is a risk of their being subjective and exclusive.

Lack of Community Participation

One common feature shared by successful language revitalization projects throughout the world is a high level of community involvement and a sense of community ownership in the school. We have not yet achieved that at Leupp School. We may have to overcome a bit of history first. As survivors of the Bureau of Indian Affairs (BIA) boarding schools, many parents in Leupp still view the school as a closed shop. We aim to change this perception through the increased presence of Navajo language and culture in the school, the introduction of the Cultural Centre, and a more pronounced effort to invite parents and community leaders into the school as consultants, volunteers, and mentors in classrooms and on curriculum development committees and parent councils.

A House Divided
When the idea of a bilingual programme was first presented to the Leupp staff, about a third of the teachers and staff were in favour of it, a third vehemently opposed it, and a third were unsure. There were many meetings and discussions, some of them heated. Opponents expressed a sincere concern that Navajo children needed to improve their English if they were going to succeed, especially since the state graduation exam, Arizona's Instrument for Measuring Success (AIMS), is only offered in English. Since the implementation of the programme, most of the 'undecideds' have joined the proponents, but opposition to the programme continues, although in more subtle ways.

Puente de Hózhó School

However, despite the difficulties experienced, the Navajo immersion programme at Leupp was so promising that we decided to provide an opportunity for students living off the reservation in the Flagstaff area to learn Navajo as well. As a result, in the fall of 2001, we started Puente de *Hózhó* School (literally, 'Bridge of Beauty'), based on our experiences at Leupp and trying to abide by a more traditional immersion model. Puente is a bilingual magnet school that offers two parallel programmes, a Spanish/English dual language programme and a Navajo immersion programme. We offered immersion instruction in three kindergarten classes in the fall of 2001, and in 2002 expanded to kindergarten and first grade.

Duration

Today, Navajo is taught for 90 per cent of the day in kindergarten, and for 80 per cent of the day in first grade. Next year (2003/4), second graders will be taught for 70 per cent of the day in Navajo, with 60 per cent for third graders in the fall of 2004, and balancing out to 50/50 instruction in fourth grade in 2005. We plan to add an additional grade each year until we serve students in grades K-12.

The response has been overwhelming. Parents call our school to put their one-year-olds on our waiting list. At *Puente de Hózhó* we had had the advantage of building the school and the programme from scratch, literally, so we were able to hire only those individuals who supported (and felt passionately about) the programme.

The project proposal was approved for funding in 1997 for a project to run for five years, while the Navajo Immersion Programme was actually introduced in fall 1998 and is still ongoing. **Funding/Budget**

In the North American spring of 1997, we applied for and were awarded a US$1.5 million Title VII grant from the U.S. Department of Education to develop a Navajo/English bilingual programme. In the fall of 1999, the proposal to create a Navajo Cultural Center to be constructed on the grounds of Leupp Public School was presented. The Flagstaff Unified School District committed US$30,000 to the project.

Leupp Public School and Flagstaff Unified School District **Responsible organizations and institutions**

Michael Fillerup **Contact**
NAU
Flagstaff
Arizona
E-mail: mfilleru@flagstaff.apscc.k12.az.us

UNITED STATES: INTERCULTURAL EDUCATION PROGRAMME

Sarah Chapple-Sokol and Kate McDermott

Type of programme and educational level	Social studies and English curriculum for students in Grades 7 – 12
Geographical and administrative level	Eastern Massachusetts region for In-School Programming; north-eastern United States reach through participation in the Northeast Regional Conference on the Social Studies, organized yearly; national reach with free-of-charge on-line curriculum resources
Indigenous target groups	Non-indigenous students in regions stated above, whose studies are enriched by exchange visits from indigenous people/students from Kenya (Maasai), Brazil (Yanomami), and India (Adivasi), by working with native people in the United States (Haudenosaunee, Iroquois, Alaska Natives and Native Hawaiians) and indigenous-led initiatives
Description of programme **Summary**	Information regarding indigenous history and culture is lacking within social studies curriculum in the United States. Educators and scholars affiliated with Cultural Survival often comment that indigenous peoples, who comprise the vast majority of the approximately 5,000 cultures and languages in the world, are either excluded

or misrepresented in most middle and high school materials. The CS Education Programme seeks to fill this gap through curriculum resources, student connections to indigenous-led initiatives through our In-School Programme, and teacher-training workshops.

The Cultural Survival Education Programme seeks to include the history, voice, and experience of indigenous peoples in the social studies and English curriculum of students in Grades 7 – 12. This will provide students with a more holistic education, expose them to the human diversity of the world, and ultimately foster their growth as global citizens. This compliments Cultural Survival's mission to promote the rights, voices, and visions of indigenous peoples.

MISSION OF CULTURAL SURVIVAL

Cultural Survival is dedicated to promoting the rights, voices and visions of indigenous peoples.

The diversity of cultures around the world is increasingly endangered due to the use of violence, forced resettlement, and pressures to assimilate. This diversity constitutes the wealth of all humanity. We, the global community, have more than a moral obligation to respect and promote cultural diversity – it is in our own self-interest.

Cultural Survival has come to think of this diversity as the 'ethnosphere', the sum total of all thoughts, beliefs, myths, and intuitions brought into being by the human imagination. Tragically, just as the biosphere is being severely eroded, so too is the ethnosphere, and at a far greater rate. It is not change that threatens the ethnosphere; it is power. Dynamic living cultures are being destroyed because of political and economic decisions made by outside entities. That such conflicts result from deliberate choices made by humans is both

Background:
legal-political,
socio-economic,
educational and
linguistic situation

discouraging and empowering. If people are the agents of cultural loss, we can also be the facilitators of cultural survival (Wade Davis, Cultural Survival Board Member and National Geographic Explorer in Residence).

Objectives and focus   To bring the rights, voices and visions of indigenous peoples into classroom discussions of history and contemporary society.

FUTURE GOALS

The programme hopes to reach more students by increasing the scope of the Secondary Schools Programme. Plans are currently under way to offer more In-School Student programmes and teacher workshops, and to increase the availability and number of curriculum resource packets. Cultural Survival also hopes to reach these goals by developing an on-line database of materials, pursuing relationships with more area schools and educators across New England, connecting more schools to indigenous-led initiatives through the Indigenous Action Network, and bringing exceptional students to the Strengthening Haudenosaunee American Relations through Education (SHARE) farm in upstate New York to learn more about Native American issues by spending time with the Haudenosaunee people.

Participation   Over the past thirty years Cultural Survival has developed a strong network of partnering institutions and more than 3,000 members who are committed to acting as a community of individuals and organizations concerned with indigenous rights.

These partnering institutions include the National Geographic Society, The Programme on Non-Violent Sanctions and Cultural Survival at the Center for

International Affairs at Harvard University, and the United Nations Permanent Forum on Indigenous Issues.

COLLABORATIVE EFFORTS

Cultural Survival, first and foremost, collaborates with indigenous peoples on all educational endeavours. For each new topic, the Secondary Schools Programme engages an indigenous group to act as consultants to ensure accuracy of indigenous perspectives in the curriculum and to provide speakers for the conferences or training sessions.

Bringing local students and indigenous peoples together not only builds awareness of indigenous issues but also helps break down stereotypes while promoting an appreciation of the diverse cultures within our own communities.

Curriculum resource packets provide educators with quality content they can use to create their own lesson plans and activities. Within each curriculum resource, we suggest activities and methods to incorporate indigenous perspectives into existing coursework, creating a flexible yet useful structure. **Methods used**

The Cultural Survival Education Programme works with contacts involved in indigenous-led initiatives that exist prior to the Education Programme's involvement. Students who learn about indigenous cultures are encouraged to become active participants in the indigenous group's self-determined projects. Action and advocacy enables students to make a positive difference in the lives of indigenous groups.

Currently there is only capacity to offer the programming in English, with some exceptions. For instance, at the Yanomami students' conference, the Yanomami and **Language(s) of instruction**

Pro-Yanomami Commission Education Coordinator spoke to the students in Portuguese, which was then translated into English. Students who attended the conference who were either Brazilian or Portuguese were able to communicate directly with the guests without a translator. Unfortunately, we do not have the capacity for simultaneous translation.

Curriculum Resource Packets

Curriculum/Themes

Curriculum resource packets, compiled and written by Cultural Survival staff in collaboration with indigenous contacts, provide teachers with the resources to guide students through the complexities of the indigenous world. Curricula are designed to cater to students in Grades 7 – 12, and are both applicable and complementary to Massachusetts and National education standards. Cultural Survival is in a unique position to develop these packets because of ongoing contact with researchers and indigenous groups. To date, Cultural Survival has created two curriculum packets, which pertain to the Maasai of Kenya and indigenous peoples of the rainforest.

The curriculum resource packets are flexible by design and easily adapted into a variety of subjects. They fit most congruently with Social Studies, History and English Language Arts.

Teacher Training Workshops

Teachers/Training

Since 2001, Cultural Survival has offered teacher-training workshops to assist educators in their desire to teach material on indigenous peoples and issues.

Workshops are held based on the number of teachers interested and are offered yearly at the Northeast Regional Conference of the Social Studies.

At each training session, we strive to include indigenous peoples as speakers and representatives of the culture being discussed. When participating in our training sessions, indigenous speakers help to co-facilitate discussion and answer a variety of questions. Most importantly, they are able to talk about their culture from an insider's perspective – and pass along this knowledge to teachers, who in turn bring that knowledge to their students.

IN-SCHOOL STUDENT PROGRAMMES AND STUDENT CONFERENCES

Materials and activities

The In-School Student Programmes and Student Conferences give students and educators a chance to actively engage in indigenous issues, through indigenous projects, and interactive curriculum, and visits by indigenous speakers. The schedule and activities of the day-long events can be tailored to individual school needs and interests through the more flexible individual school programming. A new programme, The Indigenous Action Network, will provide students with the opportunity to explore indigenous life and culture through on-line discussions with indigenous groups.

Outcomes

The Cultural Survival Education Programme has been quite successful in connecting local high-school students to indigenous groups and in promoting advocacy. Inspired by the November 2002 Conference entitled *Yanomami: Achieving Autonomy through Education*, high-school students throughout the Boston (Mass.) region, augmented by individual donors, successfully raised over US$3,500 for the Yanomami computer project. As a result, five Yanomami communities will each have one computer, which will be set up in solar-equipped health posts. These students and individuals have not only made a direct impact on the Yanomami communities but have also set the course for Yanomami-student interaction.

At the conference, held on 4 November 2002, students had the opportunity to meet with three extraordinary Yanomami teachers to learn about Yanomami culture. After learning about the incredible programmes the Yanomami have set up to ensure their own cultural survival, most student classes decided to take part in a fund-raising effort for the Pro-Yanomami Commission's (CCPY) Education Project.

As part of the Spring 2003 Maasai In-School Student Programme, students from Martha's Vineyard (Mass.) Regional High School donated more than 1,500 textbooks, encyclopedias, novels, and workbooks for the Maasai Education Discovery School in Narok, Kenya.

These types of student-led projects are at the heart of Cultural Survival's mission and reflect the ability of students to internalize the programme's message and then put this new knowledge into action.

Lessons learnt: strengths and weaknesses

Cultural Survival's education programme did not come into being effortlessly. For a few years, the education programme embodied the inspiration of whoever was the current educational director. Unfortunately, as the programme changed hands it did not grow but merely changed directions. Consequently, although both time and effort were earnestly applied to education programmes in the past, it is only now that the education programme has been organized to flourish, so that current efforts build upon past allowing the programme to both take root and extend its reach.

Duration

The programme began in 1995 and has been running ever since.

Funding/Budget

Each year, the Education Program costs Cultural Survival US$71,000, which is funded by unsolicited donations of Cultural Survival membership and subsidized by restricted grants. The Josephine Bay Paul and C. Michael Paul Foundation has consistently funded the Education Program with a generous grant of US$20,000 each year for a period of four years.

Cultural Survival

Responsible organizations and institutions

Lisa Matthews
Cultural Survival
Education Programme
215 Prospect St.
Cambridge, MA 02139
Tel: + 1 617-441-5413
E-mail: lmatthews@cs.orgwww.cs.org

Contact